# Untouched Silences

DAVID JAFFIN

First published in the United Kingdom in 2016 by
Shearsman Books
50 Westons Hill Drive
Emersons Green
Bristol BS16 7DF

Shearsman Books Ltd Registered Office
30–31 St. James Place, Mangotsfield, Bristol BS16 9JB
*(this address not for correspondence)*

www.shearsman.com

ISBN 978-1-84861-375-1

Distributed for Shearsman Books in the U. S. A.
by Small Press Distribution, 1341 Seventh Avenue, Berkeley, CA 94710
E-Mail orders@spdbooks.org
www.spdbooks.org

*Production, composition, & cover design:* Edition Wortschatz, a service of
Neufeld Verlag, Schwarzenfeld/Germany
E-Mail info@edition-wortschatz.de, www.edition-wortschatz.de

*Title picture:*
*Paul Seehaus, Dame mit Fächer, 1914.*
*Photography: Reni Hansen – ARTOTHEK*

Printed in Germany

# Contents

5

11

13

17

With continuing thanks to
Marina Moisel
for the preparation of
this manuscript

For me good poetry has always meant a unity between sound, sense, image and idea – a prevading mood-tonality. There must never be a word too many – poetry as the art of compression, "saying the most by using the least". The main adversary is cliché – using words the way they've been usually used. Poetry should take-on a cleansing function, letting words and the context-of-words shine again as newly-minted coins. Every poet tends to have his own clichés, his own oft half-routine ways of expression. These must be discovered and eliminated. Such "contaminated" poems are those ca. a quarter-of-the-whole which will be discarded.

My poetry actually "began" through a reading Wallace Stevens gave at the YMHA in New York in the early 1950s – the best of these poems such as *13 Ways of Looking at a Blackbird, The Idea of Order at Key West, 2 Letters* (in *Poems Posthumous*), *Peter Quince at the Clavier, The Snowman* … were republished in the excellent obituary on Stevens which appeared in *Time Magazine*. I sent Stevens some of my earliest poems and he responded with words I'll never forget: "You must be your own hardest critic." I've always taken those words to heart. Aside from these particular poems of Stevens the central influence on my poetry has continued to remain those great adagios of Joseph Haydn, where space, measure, and sound derive a lasting unity-of-sense.

My earliest books are generally of a quality which continues to satisfy my own aesthetic sense, they were very deliminated in theme. After years of devoting myself to another calling, that of preaching and writing about Jesus the Jew (via the Old Testament) in post-Auschwitz Germany, poetry suddenly and unexpectedly overcame me on a train to Dortmund in 1989. Ever since then, and especially in the 21st century, I've become perhaps the most prolific of poets, and that in my aging years. Why?

Because of the many-interior-tensions within my very-being and also because of my depth of interest and education in various fields. Those tensions, so explicit in my poetry are between The Christian and The Jew, between being an American and a German, between an active and an interior religious life, between time and timelessness … I am a very one-sided person, but those fields I've made my-own I've depthed as well as I could: literature, classical music, art, faith and religion, the nature of history, human understanding, love, nature, animal-life, aging and death …

The poetic process is for me at least two fold: either words come over me and demand a word discovery of their true sense; or ideas on this or that linger in my mind until they can find poetic expression. This is the more difficult for me. The ambiguity of language, open endings, levelled meanings seemingly "contradictory" sense of meaning are characteristic of my intuitively conceived poetry. Each poem should be read at least two or three times, and once, at least, aloud, to discover their intrinsic musicality.

I want to thank my dear wife of 52 years, Rosemarie, my muse, for that love, which is at the essence of my very being.

*David Jaffin*

P. S. I've often been asked why I break words be-
tween lines. As Lenore, one of my most perceptive
readers said, "You don't really break words between
the lines, but place them within the entire rhythmic
flow of the poem."

As my poems are extremely condensed I don't
want words, especially the longer ones, to be "hang-
ing out", therefore this very musical need for such a
continuing on. Word-break, if one wants to call it
that, means that these words must be put back to-
gether again, almost as if they've become recreated,
newly realized.

# From Augsburg (3)

### a) That beggar

beside St. Nicho

laus crouch
ing into the

humbling depth
of his lost–

from self-be
ing.


### b) The Town Hall (Augsburg 16 c.)

The golden
townhall so

representat
ional as if

man could blind–
himself to the

depth of his
lower mostly

self-prevading–
instinct

s.

*c) Prophetic windows*

*(Augsburg Cathedral 12 c.)*

finely orna
mental as if

their voice
s couldn't

break–through
their last

ing glass–ap
pearance

s.


## This train

landscap
ing a world

all–its–own
escaping

those fict
ive finalit

ies of time
d appearan

ces.

## Joseph Roth

always on–
the-move in

habiting
more the touch

ed-feeling
s of his own

express
ive sensibil

ity than those
interchange

able room
s of nameless

(even timeless
ly) left-be

hind
s.


## He'd lost

the sense of
his own name

lessly aban
doned to a

world of fic
tive promis

ings.

## Only women

true to their
own calling

can realize
a homed–sanct

uary with per
manent "land

ing-right
s".


## 1938 cut-down

wood grained
in-to the

searching
depth of his

time-impend
ing fear

s.


## Naked poem

s stripped to
the indelible

mark of their
no–wheres–

but-now.

*For Rosemarie'*

s softly evas
ive eyes left

his lasting im
pression of

sea-waved e
choing

s.


*Hopper a*

loned me in
to those in

escapable
silence

s of his.


*Smooth-sur*

facing Illmen
see's self–

enveloping
wind–felt en

closure
s.

29

## Night-color

> s only appar
> ently there
>
> hidden from
> the self-dis
>
> closing depth
> of their own
>
> mysterious
> source.


## Wind-fragran

> ces as light
> as spring'
>
> s transpar
> ently sensed–
>
> appeal
> s.


## Bells resound

> ing the heart
> of Munich's
>
> Marienplatz
> pulsing those
>
> silver–tone
> sounds of its

vastly unheard
medievally-

reassuring
soul.


## Modigliani *(6)*

### a) *Girl with braids (1913)*

as if the shall
owing echo of

those time-per
sisting eye

s could regain
the braided in

nocence of her
youthfully in-

felt appear
ance.


### b) *Portrait of Lunia Czechowska (1919)*

The classical
elegance of

her elongating
Brancusi-like

appearance
withholding

a most woman
ly-proud eter

nal-abstract
ion.

*c) Young Girl (1918)*

more "mother"
than girl

composing a
time-stilled

self-enclos
ing appear

ance.


*d) Naked Woman with necklace (1917)*

more like a
secular rosary

secretly fin
gered to those

most-intimate
of serene con

templation
s.


*e) Portrait of Jeanne Hébuterne (1919)*

with her vastly
self-assuming

eyes looking
down-in-

through her
soul-like com

posure.

*f) Many of Modigli*

ani's late portr
aits stylized

to an anony
mously abstract

ed sense of
non-person.


*g) Man with Pipe (1918)*

's long-lean
hat-sailored

look as if 2$^{nd}$
mating Melville'

s (Stubbs')
pipe-explor

ing pleasure
s.

## Daylight saving's time

What-ever
happened

to that o
ther-hour

a timeless
void a cosm

ic eclipse a
no-time star

ing-us-in
spaceless

ly-there.


## As if a ri

ver could two-
direction

(ed) flowing
at-the-same-

time(d) sensed-
order of only-

here mostly-
now.

## Beck symphonies (2)

### a) Beck symphonies mid 1760s (quick mvts.)

Caught haunt
ingly off-balan

cing a petul
ant sudden

ness of never-
heard-that-

one-before.


### b) Beck symphonies (slow mvts.)

thread-bare
as if reluct

antly called-
out of a spac

ed timeless
ness.


## High-timed

last yellow
ed leave

s a late autum
nal sun-ful

filling naked
ly-rehears

ed.

*Rarely seen*

such a young
ish girl–

like primly-
dressed accom

odating–smile.


*Picasso'*

s drawing
s only scarce

ly–sensed
space–elongat

ings.


*This dark*

self–enduring
silence brood

ing–through
other–sensed.

# Painting

s within paint
ings as a

play within
a play

ing-out not
so remotely-

familiar
scenario

s.

# Dehumanized (2)

a) when portrait

s become ab

stract form
s of only

pre-conceived
fleshless

appearance
s.

*b) Such "dehum*

anized" portr

aits as if
the painter

himself the
ultimate

creator of
lifeless pro

totypes.


*Only the warm-*

blooded can
fully life-

out a world
of danger

ously inhabit
ing self-call

ings.


*Aristotle'*

s "middle
way" (however

true) still
sounds more

like book-
shelved treat

ises yellow
ing those most

ly time-indul
gent page

s.


## "Giving-in-to-oneself"

as if that
other-one

couldn't be
called-in

(as well)
for a safe

ly-satisfying
life-journ

ey.


## Freud

only three-de
mensioned

those multi-
personed self-

exceeding
life-spanned.

## Car-light

> s search
> ing the night'
>
> s irretriev
> able phantom
>
> ed–depth.


## Is day-time

> a renewed life–
> time(d) from
>
> the midst of
> night's self–
>
> precluding
> depthed–dark
>
> nesses.


## Little puff

> ed–up left–o
> ver cloud'
>
> s morning an
> awakening
>
> sense of in
> nocently touch–
>
> felt find–me–
> there
>
> s.

*Beck*

    primitive
    ly rough-ed

    ged explosive
    ly storm-and-

    stressed for mo
    ments of short-

    edged branch-
    sketched inter

    ludes.


*Those time-*

    faced autumn
    al shadow

    ings left
    the sky na

    kedly leaf
    ed of its

    open-sensed
    light-last

    ing colored-
    down impress

    ions.

*That secretly*

    self-kept com

    posured cat in
    digenously

    (but scarce
    ly decipher

    able) claw
    ed silence

    s.


*This floor*

    now imperson
    ally stone-

    hard that his
    feet left

    little impres
    sions on its

    own timeless
    certitude.


*On the his*

    torical when
    these soft-

    phrasing
    waves slowly

    accumulate
    after-thought

s continuous
ly felt–

through
their oncom

ing silence
s.


## A lone

street–light
in–the–midst

of a shift
ing sea of un

touchable
darkness

es.


## This rail

ing cool and
closely–touch

ed his embrac
ing hand to

the pulse of
their blood–en

compassing
brightness

es.

## Night-wind

    s darkly inhab
iting a depth

    of unexplor
ed silence

    s.


## Beck's

    storm-and-
stress punct

    uating syllab
les of a mo

    mentary life-
surge.


## His so fluent

    ly compelling
friendli

    ness hidden
within a pois

    oned snake-
like urge to

    strike fang
ed-deep.

*Brancusi'*

s bronzes
left an im

plicit touch–
shine of shall

ow autumnal
breath-space.


*This late*

autumnal
bloomed-scent

more a depth
of dying

light-exposure
s.


*Those hidd*

en inexplicit
motives we

so slyly im
ply of o

thers may bely
an unravel

ling of our
own cloth-in

folding intent
ions.

## Charles

Seliger's
color–depth

ed earth ex
posures of

(as yet) un
explored

(though per
sistently)

self-incall-
ings.


## Charles'

bow-tied
smile as ex

plicitly self–
satisfying

as the finish
ing surface

s of his al
ways brightly–

colored sound–
appeal

s.

## Klee'

s Rose Garden
44 climbing

scented–pass
ages of a

city's bloom
ing-colored

fullness
es.


## Poems from Cyprus

When appear
ance-sake be

comes person-
sake all made-

up to the new
est fashion'

s mirroring
modes of self-

deception.

*This land'*

s so dried-
down that e

ven the spar
sam trees

seem as if
embarrass

ingly self-in
habiting.


*Cactus-*

land stone-
thirsting

its bristl
ing blood

less-source.


*Scrubbed*

shadows too
low-down to

signal more
than a modest

ly inhabit
ing self-con

tentment.

## Here only

the dark speak
s with a voice

of its own un
explored si

lence
s.


## Rephrasings

Only if it'
s been said

before rephras
ing its not-al

ways samed
self-attune

ment
s.

## Even here

in the farth
est reach of

summer's all-
consuming time

lessness
leaves fall

ing the color
ed-edge of

their autumn
al in-spoken

sadness
es.


## A poet's

lasting heri
tage echoing

its still lone
ly unredeem

ed (though
through-touch

ed) evoking
silence

s.

*A sudden-*

bird left be
hind only a

stopped–mo
ment's color

ings.


*Lost poetic-*

years now fully
realizing

their unharves
ted (though

grained–ripe)
withholding

s.


*English*

the most
forth–right

(and yet)
secretly un

rehearsed
of all those

time–inhabit
ing language

s.

*These soft*

ly-evasive
semi-tropi

cal breeze
s scarce

ly-touched
(though in

timately
sensed–

through) ap
pearance

s.


*Newly re*

called descript
ive wording

s may also
harbour e

lusively un
revealing

innuendo
s.

*Morning a*

wakens as if
untouched

from its dark
ly-celestial

dream-seclud
ing reverie

s.


*Sturdy youth*

ful trees grow

th Cyprus'
time-securing

historical-
replentish

ings.


*Wave-expanse*

s sun-lit dis

tancing those
time-forgott

en remembran
ces.

## These cool-

refreshing wa
ter the very-

depth of his
soulled self-

searching
quietude

s.


## Memoried (3)

### a) Medieval

Jew-treasure
s buried at

a depth be
yond the blood-

range of their
earthed-down

silence
s.


### b) Cyprus

harbour
ing the fear

ed-memorie
s of those

turned-back
emptied-dream

s.

*c) A house*

left-behind
blood-forsak

ening its
still haunt

ed-memorie
s.


*If (as Calder (3)*

    *a) on believed)*

that "man's
greatest sin

birthed to
live"-out

the untold
beauties of a

world banish
ed from the

true-light
of an ever-

dawning fu
ture.

*b) If "life'*

s but a dream"
(Caldéron)

then all we'
ve ever-known'

s but an un
resolving

darkness.


*c) Prince Siges*

mund (Caldéron)
so firmly

chained-in
castle-ston

ed an untouch
able height

from his self–
devastat

ing instinct
s.

## Only if we

can learn (a
gainst our

very-being)
to witness

ourselves
s in those

we need op
press.


## This island-realm *(after Shakespeare)*

If an earth
ly paradise

could harbour
the tideful

source of our
most in-dwell

ing fear
s.

## America'

s refuged-
shores now

soiled with
the claims of

its own para
disical mythed-

source
s.


## Pathway

s (though
scarcely de

cipherable)
high-above

the sea's
echoing rest

lessly through
our own pulsed-

sensed being.

## Identity poems (3)

### a) Child-transport (late 1930s)

She didn't
really know

who she was
awoke years

later to a
nother world

than of accust
omed there-be

ing an other
wise-self as if

not always the
samed-one.


### b) She couldn'

t find her real
war-time father

(ed) by an un
known being a

most real part
of her own

life's blood-
line.

*c) Adopted (as*

he later-
learned)

from an un
known parent

age as if a
foreign–being

to his own
self–exclus

ive source.


## These island

ed low–sense
roofs bloom

ing–over
flowering

self–apprais
als.

## Display (2)

*a) Even here*

the fallen
blossoms

earthed with
a light less-

shadowing
scent of un

timely dis
play.


*b) Tattoo*

ed a bodied-
stigma skinn

ed to the
muscular

depth of er
rant-display.


## Those who

can't listen
to silence

will never
realize their

most intimate
sound-puls

ed very-be
ing.

*Their incess*

> ant-need for
> rhyme as wave
>
> s rowed-in
> to a routine
>
> of evenly-
> placed word–
>
> sense.


*Leaves here*

> light-consum
> ing the fatal
>
> grasp of death'
> s time-encom
>
> passing hold.


*Games-like*

> Life-game
>
> s played-out
> on a chess–
>
> board's pre–
> figuring
>
> hand
> s.

*Winter-games* (after Breughel)

Winter-game
s children'

s sport-like i
mitation

s other par
ent's dream–

sourced time–
play.


*Calderón'*

s dramas (how
ever deeply–

sensed) (even
their allus

ive dream–
play)-ing

out a world a
woken from its

lost illusion–
like reverie

s.

*Spain's*

>warrior-past
>landscap
>
>ing its rough
>ly-hewed indig
>
>enously-heroic
>time-sequen
>
>ces.

*Calderón'*

>s "Life is but
>a Dream"
>
>Only a woman'
>s warmth could
>
>soften Sigismund'
>s heathed-firm
>
>ed blood-in
>stinct
>
>s.

## Goya

two-sided
(heart and

mind) Spain'
s decaydent

eclipse though
his always-read

ied-eye clear-
faced.


## After

shadowing
birds more

wind's sound-
sensing

s.


## Jewell-

eyed secret
ly intent

light-expos
ures.

# Night

winds only
sourced–

through the
dark of un

timely dis
tancing

s.


## Medieval Icon-paintings *(3)*

*a) Medieval*

icon–paint
ings more a

spiritual
tradition of

same–sourced
prayered–color

ings.

*b) Medieval*

icon-paining
s created less

through the
form of mind-

exposure
s than by

the inner
quiet of pray

ered contemplat
ions.


*c) Medieval icon-*

painting
s the sound-

scope of time
less prayer

ed-echoing
s.


## *Flowering*

branches color
ed his mind-

sense with in
explicitly-

formed remem
brance

s.

*Why are*

>these light-in
>herent star
>
>s awakened at
>less-apparent
>
>time-sequence
>s.

*Now even time*

>less truths
>have become
>
>dated with
>their repeat
>
>edly sanct
>ioned-invocat
>
>ions.

*She left*

>him with an
>after-taste
>
>of most unplea
>santly-taint
>
>ed thought-
>feeling
>
>s.

## Here most

ly theoreti
cal snakes

pictured large
in poisonous

imitative-
poses.


## Quick flash-

eyed indigen
ous hunter

s scanning
these island

ed ravine
s for flee

ing hare-foot
ed soundless

ly scarcely-
scented impress

ions.

## Mountain

ous Cyprus'
plunging

heights in
to the stone–

echoing depth
s of its

timeless
ly ravenous

deeps.


## A deserted village (after Oliver Goldsmith)

left voice
lessly intact

inhabited
only by a

bandoned hous
es and the

narrow street
s of a still-e

choing past.

*When the*

poem-pulse
inks itself

out in self-
reclaiming

thought-in
terval

s.


*However wide*

ly-scoped this
islanded land-

length alway
s the self-

surrounding
sea's incess

antly-alert
timeless-re

calling
s.


*For Rosemarie'*

s peace-making
eyes the soft

ly compelling
now-as-alway

s love-nourish
ings.

*Faces-of-the-*

    dead looming so
    presently-a

    live evoking
    memories of

    their long–
    gone apparent

    ly-now.


*This sea teem*

    ing with the

    invisible
    life of sound

    lessly muted-
    shadowing

    s.


*Church Panagia Angeloktisti (3)*

    *a) John the Baptist's (13th c.)*

    almost bodi
    less eyes

    searching be
    yond life's e

    lusive time–
    span.

*b) Saint John the Theologian' (16<sup>th</sup> c.)*

s bare-foot
ed silence

s expressive
ly self-tran

ced.


*c) Mosaic of Mary, Jesus and Archangel (6<sup>th</sup> c.)*

classical
ly embracing

(though inward
ly withhold

ing) time
less-sequenc

es.


## Decorative

white-bloss
omings a

speechless
land's flow

ering instin
cts.

## Taxi-driver *(2)*

*a) His rapid-*

motion gun–
like talk–in

centives viv
idly recall

ing my own
still shadow

ing past.


*b) Few today*

(as he)

seek–out the
self reviving

spiritual
source of

these ancient
church–enclos

ing time–quiet
udes.

*Is the re*

petitive warm
th of each

sun–consuming
day but a time

less copy of
our own self–

certifying
shadowless

interval
s.


*These cool*

waters immer
sing his bodi

ful being re
freshing

ly self–sancti
fied.


*Each touch-*

selective
word a time

ful mosaic
of pre-form

ing instinct
ive color

ings.

## Rosemarie'

s time-invok
ing eye's sub

tlely-soul
ed express

iveness.


## The Judge of Zalamea (Caldéron) (7)

a) A truly demo

cratic society
stands well-a

bove class dis
tinction

s and even demo
cratically-

espoused theor
etical-façade

s.


b) Why is a wo

man's honor

blemished
if she's help

lessly mis
used.

*c) Is lust the*

bastard–father
of love's e

ven selfless
ly all–en

compassing
desire

s.


*d) Why should*

a misused wo
man claim last

ing–satisfact
ion by marry

ing the scound
rel who so-read

ily abused
her.


*e) Crespo the*

farmer–judge

more the al
most perfect

image of what'
s rarely true–

to-life.

*f) If (as Crespo*

felt) once–

a–farmer al
ways–a–far

mer why could
he display a

wisdom at
least the e

qual of a
pure–blooded

nobleman.


*g) Was it real*

ly a crime
of Juan (Cres

po's son)
(although only

a farmer) to at
tack the man

who raped his
sister and

strung–up his
father (indeed

an officer of
the king's

forces).

*Branched-*

    flowers contin
    ually falling

    (even here)
    through the

    saddened
    claims of au

    tumnal death–
    calling

    s.


*The unexpect*

    ed (as a strange
    ly colored

    bird) branch
    ed–in the

    thicket of a
    timeless

    self–denial.

## A dream

less sleep
sea-calming

almost untouch
ably smoothed–

in self-expand
ing reflect

ions.


## Good poem

s (although

playing the
same field

s) may impli
citly quest

ion those
most-firm

ly establish
ed rules-of-

the-game.


## Little child

ren may eye in
expressible

truths Adoles
cents sense

their blood-
streamed ori

gin while poets
touch-sense

their immuta
ble word-phras

ings.


## The narrow

urgings of
these bare-

branched mo
ments reach

ing to the in
escapable

grasp of leaf
ed-continuit

ies.


## Zoo-visit (14)

*a) Flamingo*

s slender
ly balanc

ing mostly up
lifting

thought
s.

*b) Over-sized*

peacocks treed–
down though

crowned–up
with up-end

ing over–
sight

s.


*c) Kangaroo*

s hastily as
piring two–

footed spring–
jump

s.


*d) The blue*

peacock's
dressed–out

in ceremon
ial celest

ial star–
glancing

s.

*e) The statues*

que lion rest
lessly reclaim

ing its dark
ly–inhabit

ing jungle-
instinct

s.


*f) The lioness'*

womanly e
mancipating

soul-vista
s.


*g) Giant tur*

tles perman
ently housed

in their pre–
designed

slow-down
comfort

s.

*h) Fishing-cat*

stared me in
to those ob

selete water
s of glass

ed–perspect
ives.


*i) Gazelle'*

s lyrical
ly-fleet

ing fragile
silence

s.


*j) They can't*

monkey-me in
to their up

ending hide–
out smile

s.

*k) Zebra*

s unconscious
ly-stripped

for locat
ing self-suffi

cience
s.


*l) Sea-lion'*

s heavily as
tute slippery

watering-ex
posure

s.


*m) Penguin*

s coolly sold
iering their

slow-footed
up-right ex

pressive
ness.

*n) The Pavian'*

s rock-sitt
ing its self–

conscious
ly beautify

ing presen
ce.


## He didn't

fit-so-well
into Midas'

worn-down
clothes

couldn't e
ven dollar-

and-cent his
lesser money-

minded instin
cts.


## Open-aired

almost as a
puppet string

ed to other-
handed space-

down pulling
s.

## Roads now

strangely
and distant

ly alone land
scaping with

out the touch–
feel of an e

choing-respon
se.


## Personae *(6)*

*a) It was like*

going-to-the
zoo with Uncle

Phil imitat
ing all the a

nimal noise
s caged-in

(as well)
his own in

stincts for o
ther woman

ly softness
es.

*b) Aunt Debby*

his beauteous
wife locked–

herself-in on
the wedding

night from Phil'
s avaracious

instinctual
feel–find

s.


*c) Aunt Gertie'*

s pointer's
finger(ed) e

ven–beyond a
ministerial

length of be
havioral re

straint
s.

*d) Uncle Julius*

free-float
ing as a solem

nal Jew-fish
surfacing

Gertie's e
ver-invoking

admonishion
s with his un

duly-outlast-
ing smile.


*e) Little Sammy*

fancied his
lesser cerebrial

functioning
s with match

ing-clothes
and a sport-

streamed car-
timed exclus

iveness.

*f) Oar-fish*

(that most do
cile of creat

ures) simply
floating the

increasing
length of his

undiscover
ing body.


*Madame Kobold* *(Calderón) (6)*

*a) darkly pur*

suing a for

bidden life
at–the–o

ther–side–of–
self.


*b) Cosme (a*

servant) imag
inatively in

habited by all
those superst

itions that
oft accompany

the–other–side–
of–faith.

*c) That two-sid*

ed glassed-
cabinet as

life's ready
one-way-open

ing to a no-
ways-out.


*d) Caldéron*

soldier adven
turer lady's

man and priest
a more than

two ways in-
and-out-of

life's alway
s-alternat

ing reflect
ing-surface

s.


*e) When honor*

becomes the
only lasting

measure of
one's God-giv

en life-time
performanc

es.

*f) What is and*

what appears–
to-be each

shadowing
more–of–us

than we can
realize why.


## That November

morning stood–
him-out as

those vacant
trees stand

ing so still(ed)
his own lack

of such last
ing-stability.


## Grandma Guzy

even in those
sunshine sitt

ing–out–com
forts of Cen

tral–Park–West
ghettoed–for–

life in those
feared Jew-apprai

sals of what's–
coming–next.


*Deep-sea-*

fish (as most
of us) submerg

ing the dark
nesses of

those under
water seclus

ive depth-in
telling

s.


*That so-Jew*

ish–means of
smiling-at-one'

s-errant-self
the easiest

way of get
ing-out-of

those two-fac
ed enclos

ing dilemma
s.

## A soft autumn

al sky almost
equally phas

ing-out most
of life's in

herently weigh
ted-down anx

ietie
s.


## For Rosemarie

When feeling-

out how you'll
hear this poem

becomes an es
pecial part of

the poetic-pro
cess itself.


## For a poetic-

nature experien
cing can be

come (as well)
that so imagini

tively elusive
word-find.

## Lost poem

s as voiced-si
lences search

ing a way-out
from a locked-

in room's lost
key.


## It wasn't

what-she-said
(so convinc

ingly thought-
through) and

yes empathetic
ally-phrased

but even-more-
so what-she-

didn't.

## Burn-out *(for E. L.) (3)*

*a) as a candle*

lit to a

self–intens
ing glowed the-

most–intimate-
reach of its

waxed–down re
sidue

s.


*b) Burn-out as*

if forced in
to an echo

less corner'
s self–retreat

ing silence
s.


*c) Burn-out*

that speech
less emptie

d–reach sha
dowlessly

self–confin
ing.

# Lope de Vega' *(for Warren) (2)*

*a) s Fuenteovejuna*

Can a time-in
dulgent re-read

ing a play's o
therwise-intent

(ly) mirror an a
ctual part of

its own (self-
maintaining)

intrinsic mean
ings.


*b) Can critics*

even-better
than-the-au

thor-himself'
s so intuit

ively-subject
ive meaning

s.

## If "some

things would
be better-

left unsaid"
they may well

keep speaking a
loud in their

air-tight
confine

ment
s.


## Should life

become a con
tinual confron

tation with
one's-own

lasting
sense-for-

meaning.

## Sentiment

al singers
more glimmer

ing eyes and
under-ground

touched-in
flection

s flowing
self-express

ively enchant
ment

s.


## November 9

The date for
modern German

history but
for-a-Jew

only the bro
ken glass of

the broken tra
dition of 200

years of a Ger
man-Jewish

"symbiosis"
splinter

ing-reflect
ively blood-

ripe.

*Händel's*

Saul in a mod
ern semi-opera

tic mode (true
to Händel's

musical ori
gins) contrapun

tally-dramati
cally alive

to the tragedy
of a Judaic

kingdom that
would deny (David)

and fulfill
(Saul) its God–

forsaken
tradition of

its own (and
His) ever self–

invoking image.

*a) Händel too-*

little apprecia
ted in Germany

(despite Haydn'
s and Beethoven'

s judgement) per
haps because

they find him
too British

pomp-and-circum
stancy.


*b) Haydn too-*

little apprecia
ted in Germany

(despite Mozart'
s and Brahms' judg

ment) perhaps
because his

happy-positive
even humorous

view-of-life
doesn't quite

fit-in with
their tragic

sense-of-be
ing.

## A city of

glassed-wind
ows imagined

persons (if-
at-all) anony

mously sound-
resistant.


## "All aboard"

The train as
if phases-in-

life passing
through stop

s (scheduled
or not) End-

station usu
ally unexpect

edly-there.


## H. B.

She was hard-
to-place her

taste and per
soned in a

history
that kept foll

owing-her-down.

*Help need*

> ed for oppres
> sed Christian
>
> s a two-way
> street with
>
> our (more-or-
> less) empty-
>
> handed faith.

*If hats*

> talked back
> then Magritte'
>
> s stolidly
> front-facing
>
> and Macke'
> s windowed
>
> for a self-as
> suming resum
>
> mée.

*Train-sitt*

ing with time
not coming-

on but eas
ing-back

through life'
s continuing

after-flow.


*Why-is-*

it that these
isolated hous

es seem so va
cantly aband

oned to a leaf
less late-aut

umnal setting.


*Have these*

newly sky-scrap
ing cities

been risen to
a height of

time-forgott
en distanc

ings.

*Now (when*

retired) days-of-
the-week seem

to have lost
their own in

dividually-
sensed time-

scope.


*Conference for Christian Martyrs (3)*

a) *Martyrs*

We have
only become

blood-birthed
from the dark

ly-rich-soil
of their Christ-

beholden suffer
ings.

*b) Christian-*

free-zones
as those Jew-

determined
ones world but

a barren de
sert of birth

less dream
s.


*c) We who live*

the ease of
satiated

pleasures can
hardly nour

ish a world
of needful

spiritual-
growth.

*He sang his*

faith so loud
and mournful

ly tear-ripe
as if calling

its self-va
cant source

(as Saul's Sam
uel) from the

dead of his
once-apparent

dream
s.


*My dear cou*

sin David be
lieved (as

he said)
in all of the

10 Command
ments except

that first-
one embrac

ing all-of-
the-rest.

## Those who

fear to wit
ness the-source-

of-their-own-
faith may be

come (in time)
desert-dry-

at-heart.


## In Memory R. S.

He steadfast
ly proclaimed

the faith of
"the quiet

ones in land"
while remain

ing ever-so-
actively-

intent.


## Our first

(and always-
present battle

field) those so
contrary force

s deadly war-
depthed with

in ourselves
s.


## *The poet*

wields a sword
of-his-own

as Ezekiel
hard-facing

a self-deceiv
ing world at

its soul-leng
thed-end.


## *Some carpet*

s look-more-
like used-out

thought
s at the foot-

length of our
own repeated

ly stepped-
down presence.

## Corridor

s of emptied
spaces at the

dead-end of
our outlast

ing thought
s.


## Pre-determin *(3)*

*a) ed to marry a*

man of her–

own-faith but
not of her-own-

choice She es
caped abroad

to an almost
unknown self

having lost
at least

half-of-her-
own.

*b) It was a*

strange and
(at-the-first)

foreign God
who called

her to seek
refuge in Him

or remain self–
forsaken at–

the-will of
her own "for

eigned" parent
s.


*c) A dual-i*

dentity of
one streamed

in two-direct
ions though

caught at-the–
middle of no

wheres–but–
then.

# Egyptian (2)

### a) Christian

s at the

foot-fears
of their char

red-down chur
ches with only

a "homeless"
God to con

sole their va
cant sense-

of-loss.


### b) It was only

that shock-of-
loss that re

vived the
Christ-identi

ty of a church
ritualized

in an histori
cally-revered-

tradition.

## "The Jews"

> he called
> them of a
>
> people up-root
> ed from the
>
> ground-depth
> of their his
>
> torical call
> ings.

## The coming

> Luther-year
> of a church
>
> de-faced-be
> yond-recognit
>
> ion of its
> founder's
>
> Christ-script
> ed-message.

## When the

New Testament
(so-scarcely-

sourced) left
its far-better-

equipped theol
ogians to such

vastly open-
field speculat

ions.


## Smoke'

s mysterious
ly vanish

ing moment
s untoucha

bly elusive.


## Can friend

ships last
when there's

no center
where shadow

s cross-and-
touch to a

depth of speech
less response.

## When figure

s crossing si
lently into

the dark's e
choing their

unspoken in
tent for a

bloodful-sac
rifice.


## Have the dis

tant suffer
ing of name

less Christ
ians immersed

my own indwell
ing feared-si

lence
s.


## First

through-tell
ing frost'

s distinct
ive clarity-

hold.

*When winter*

takes-hold of
those bare-

branched-bird
s do their

feather
s still re

main colorful
ly in-tact.


*Cold's dis*

tinctive
ly unheard

(though time
lessly im

pressed)
wind-exposure

s.


*Leafless*

trees as if
shamed by

their naked
ly self-re

vealing de
sign

s.

*This cold-*

enclosure
d winter-

morning's
tentative

light-reveal
ings.


*The time-*

phrasing to–
and-fro of

this swing'
s rhythmi

cally trans
cending ac

cord
s.


*Dark winter*

night's so
vastly self–

assuming
worlds of un

touchably e
vasive sound

lessness.

## A little

girl's first-
spring-dress

patterned
to a touch-

feel (of per
haps) there-

I-am.


## The right (5)

a) ly-touched

held-in word

formed to its
own sense of

being only-
there of

its no-where
s-else.


b) No-poetry-

left when that
lasting-breath

of the child-
in-us succumb

s to life'
s other-time

always-need
s.

*c) Children*

sold in-to
the slavery

of a person
less being

no-wheres-
of-themselv

es.


*d) Today when*

trivial pro
saic time-

truths are
pedestall

ed as poetry-
of-the-high

est-order.


*e) Few intimate*

places left
for the breath

ful ease of
open-aired ex

pressive
ness.

*These self-*

> prevading
> late-autumn
>
> al leaf-ton
> ed interior-
>
> releasing
> darkness
>
> es.

*The Magic Flute* (Mozart) (5)

> *a) well-known*
>
> as a non-flute
>
> lover(ed)
> his most beaut
>
> eous opera in
> to those phant
>
> om-realms of
> a flute magic
>
> ally-attuned-
> to-the-most-
>
> spiritual-
> of-calling
>
> s.

*b) Mozart caught*

between an in
sensitive

church-respon
se and a Lodge

of spiritual-
brother

s show-pieced
his greatest

opera for-the-
one while an

swering his
instinctive

death-calling
s with the

Requiem(ed)-
God of-the-o

ther.


*c) Papageno*

the most natur
ally human

least dressed-
up with his

magic-fluted
bird-flutter

ing qualitie
s.

*d) The Queen-of-the-Night*

brightly star
red the myster

ious depthed-
fears of dark

nesses' other-
wordly realm

s.


*e) Even the*

orchestra
repeated

ly fluted Mo
zart's self-

concealing
love of an in

strument high-
keyed even be

yond human-re
sponse.


## Predator

tree-topped
birds clawed

the very-depth
of their blood-

descending in
stinct

s.

## This house

(relived so
many time

s) has per
soned the chang

ing modes of
my self-relin

guishing very-
being.

## A poem

often change
s-course in-

the-midst of
its still un

telling-des
tination.

## Some women

we've known at-
once sensual

ly time-keyed
(and yet)

continual
ly phrased-in

spiritual
word-invocat

ions.

## If Gide reject

ed Swann's Way

because of gram
matical irregu

larities What-
more-proof-need

ed for my
future criti

cal demeanor
s.


## Sabatina'

s no-way-out
of a closed-

society to a
freedom-in-

Christ left
her animall

ed hunted-down
death-feared

in an anony
mous room's

always-there.

*Not only the*

image of the
wandering-

Jew but Jew
ed-out time

s and place
s left God'

s chosen-one
s self-reliant

on Him alone.


*For example Mozart's Magic Flute Ouverture*

Some theme
s (especial

ly musical
ones) perpet

uate our mind
and sense

s into an orch
estra of con

tinuously-a
lert color

ing-sound
s.

# Three Poems for Lenore (3)

a) *If it's only-*

so and no–

wheres-else
(then) he's be

come worded
in-to a por

trait timeless
ly-his.


b) *The continu*

ous flow of
pre-seemed

words instinct
ively-touched

from their be
ginning's-

end.


c) *When place*

s so person
ed-alive the

when-and where
of one's re

turning-hom
ed.

*When dark be*

comes breath
lessly-sensed

Tunnelled-in
a no-where

s-out.


*When only*

words can
possibly re

trieve those
lost-moment

s echoing
still.


*Spoiled*

with too-much
goodness as

a cake cream
ed with lay

ers of time-
fulfilling

after-taste
s.

*He swallow*

ed–me–down
with more than

my Jewish na
ture could–take

defending
the needs of

the SS killer'
s calling

s.


*And then*

Haydn's great
F Minor Variat

ions horizoned
well–beyond

its own depth
ed–sanctuar

ies.


*A numbed*

leafed–down
November–

Saturday
with little–

more-to-re
late than

speechless
shadowing

s.


## Christian'

s all-too-
ready forgive

ness seems to
me often

more word-ripe
than soul-depth

ed.


## The biblical Jewish-state

(with its role-

model adulterous-
murderer King

David) was no less
unholy than its

present-day mod
el for the

Lord's oncoming
redemption.

*How have*

  these tropical
  intensely–color

  ed orchids
  been waiting-

  out the time
  less depth of

  these winter
  night's self–

  inhabiting
  darkness

  es.


*For Rosemarie'*

  s sensuous love
  at 75 with

  your beaute
  ous undress

  ed smiling
  me back-and–

  on to those
  youthful time-

  becoming plea
  sures.

## The ambigui

ties of lang
uage(s) our–

own word-stan
ced many-sided

ness.


## When Charles

realized the
money-market

for "art"
would leave

what's genu
inely aesthet

ically-his
to those side–

rooms of con
templative

passerby
s.

*Few-of-us*

left as those
seldom-es

caping Jew
s and those

who kept to-
their-own-

quiet-way
s in a world

desolate
ly-loud while

secretly blood-
intensely prom

pted.


*Lovers at*

three-quarter
s-to-the-cen

tury-mark(ed)
us the source

of where ri
vers secret

ly awakening
those soil-

depthed-through
ways.

## Jew-baited (3)

*a) He Jew-bait*

ed me time–
and–again as

if to make-
up for his

people's
resigning

guilt–source
d appearan

ces?


*b) Baited-and-*

hooked as a
brightly-color

ed fish surfa
cing the depth

of its time–
consoling con

templation
s.

*c) Why as free-*

sporting game
innocently

trapped in
to those time—

consuming
death-hold

s.


## *Et Terra Pax* (Frank Martin)

Exciting

music color
ing the out

er-limits of
clashing-ton

alities dead—
ended a too—

familiar
ity of exclu

sively repeti
tive sound-re

membranc
es.

*Bare-bran*

ched fragile
ly-touched

moment
s of sound

less on-hold
ings.


*Jiménez* (3)

*a) when word*

s find to

their
only-self.


*b) when flow*

ers scent be
yond their in-

coloring-
find

s.

*c) transcen*

dental tran
sparencie

s.

## *Home should*

never estrange-
itself from be

coming an al
ways-return.

## *Catching young*

children'
s eyes as a

fanciful
ly-strung kite

sky-bound.

## Really-good poetry *(Jiménez)*

sends-off my
eye-scheme

cloud-wander
ings.

## On Artistic-fashions

Imitation
make-up will

old-itself-
out undress

ed to a bare-
boned empti

ness.

## Maybe the

self-recall
ing depth

of these poem
s will help

a withering
(deceptive)

world's re
turn to a

still time-e
lusive sensi

bility.

*Today when*

sensuality
has become

even-more
than its self-

proclaiming
encompass

ing world-
sense.


*"Getting-even"*

more-often-
than-not put

s one at-odd
s-length from

that better-
side-of-self.


*My family*

blood-stream
s have run-

down anemical
ly-paled from

mother's grave-
stoned finali

ties.

## *Molto Adagio* *(Beethoven op. 59,2) (2)*

*a) The last word*

depthed to its
ultimate si

lences so lyri
cally compact

as if time
(and sense)

had finally
stopped there.


*b) Presto (last mvt.)*

on-the-move
as a horse

man breath
lessly aimed

at no-where
s-else than

furtively-
homed.


## *Dvořák Quartet op. 61 (2)*

*a) as if one-*

voice intimate

ly soloed to
an alway

s communal-
oneness.

*b) Apollon M.*

a young Czech-
quartet as the

Dvořák singul
arly voiced

(yet) always
accorded to a–

unity-of-sound-
sense.


*This knott (1938)*

ed-wood still
securely-in

tact though blem
ished and stain

ed-through as
if time could

remain so blood
lessly alert.

## *Those sudden*

moments when
Beethoven'

s tensioned e
ven-beyond his

most form-decisive
withholding-

power
s.


## *Reminded mo*

ments personal
ly inhabit

ing a fading
(though still

faintly ob
scured)

timeless
ness.

*They sat so-*

> firmly sound–
> intent age-in
>
> tact as if the
> concert had al
>
> ready begun
> resolute
>
> ly no-where
> s-else.


*Little bird*

> s branch–hopp
> ing their so
>
> allusive
> ly-sensed co
>
> lor-find
> s.


*Each poem*

> should leave
> us more time
>
> and space-con
> templation
>
> s.

# García Lorca (2)

*a) abstract*

ly landscap

ed through
Spain's rough-

sounding hill'
s nakedly

witness
ing-sun.

*b) García Lorca'*

s bloody-a
lert verse

shot-through
its timeless

ly imperson
ed.


# F Minor Quartet op. 20, 5 *(Haydn) (3)*

*a) Was that real*

(ly) Haydn

or a vacant re
minder of some

where lost to
untouched

(and even)
forbidden

paths.

*b) Slow move*

ment still
violin-over

telling rhap
sodically re

calling-inter
ludes (not yet)

a unison of
nowheres-else-

but-now.


*c) Final fugue*

as if call
ed from an un

touchable re
splending

depth.


## *Quartet 4* (Bartók) (3)

*a) Motorical*

ly-brash start

and ending
now cliché

s over-spok
en.

*b) that hush*

ed pizzacot
to as if se

cretly self-
escaping.


*c) The slow move*

ment (as e
ven Haydn's

op. 1) center
ed a withhold

ing-universe
of-now and

only-here.


## Quartet op. *41,3 (Schumann) (2)*

*a) That last move*

ment still on-

coming through-
timed rapid

ly self-exceed
ing.

*b) slow move*

ment romanc

ed episodic
ally dream–

tranced.


## Desirious poem

He wanted to
landscape

those slop
ing–hills–of–

her infold
ing valley'

s darkly–scent
ed earthi

ness.


## Few leave

s left a
faintly col

ored remem
brance of those

breathless
ly–touched un

recalling–mo
ment

s.

*When "the con*

science of a
nation"s a

leftish cabara
tist or a

muck-raking
novelist hid

ing behind his
Nazi past.


*We all must*

pay-a-price
for special

gifts Life's
the most pre

cious death-
scented.

## Sleep

less night
s as a cur

tain ever–so–
certainly

closed–in
those self–in

habiting rest
less interlude

s.


## Jorge Guillén *(3)*

*a) Names*

sourced to
an unknown

sameness
of word's

satisfying
ly self–find

ing.


*b) Cities*

death–haunted
stone–intens

ing life
less shadow

ings.

*c) Time may be*

come the mea
sure of all

things time
lessly self–

apparent.


## Gurlitt'

s 6<sup>th</sup> floor
darkly shadow

ing room
(ed) with Nazi

art-loot Icon
his phantom

ed lost sense
of-an-other

wise-world.


## This late

November day
as bare-sensed

as her world
downed to its

irretriev
ably confin

ed-loss.

*Vicente Aleixandre* (after Michelangelo) (2)

    *a) The word*

only become
s flesh-warm

when indescrib
ably love-

length
touched.


    *b) Hand*

the open-end
of her recept

ively bodied
longing

ness.


*Luis Cernuda* (2)

    *a) Aloned when*

truth opposi

ties its o
therwise

sense-of-be
ing inarticu

lately unfath
omed.

*b) Is love*

even–more
than death

can truly-
hold Or is

it the loss
of its youth

fully bodied-
incarnat

ion.


## Dark wind

s shadow
ing the ines

capable depth
of these emp

tied silence
s.


## Not only

animals real
ize their own

self-enclos
ing selective

area–code
s for there

(and no–where
s-else).

## Mallarmé *(from Rimbaud)*

(at the oppos
ite end)

reworded the
exact-extent

of that usual
ly-familiar

unknown.


## Haydn's reminder

a theme can
only vary

its home-bred
sanctity if

(despite irre
versible a

sides) Time-
centering.


## Beethoven's 1ˢᵗ Quartet *(first mvt.)*

all-on-its-
own sharply-de

fining its un
deniably a

cute-pre
sence.

## As those down (and dying nations)

(or even faith
s) as deeply

under-water
ed fish re-emer

ging colorful
ly-surpris

ing intact.


## Mother

(though of a
lesser-breed

herself) be
tweened a no-

wheres-other
ethically-

astute father
and a husband

pedestall
ed liberal

ly high-above
any such time-

withholding
docked-down re

servation
s.

## His-own-way

He had "his-
own-way"

they said
as if ways be

came person
ed or led to

a seemingly
otherwise-ob

trusiveness.

## "Hard-sensed"

they-called-it
as G. Martel'

s always Ver
mont-winter

ed frozen-
ground aware

ness.

## As only a De

Gaulle could
so genuine

ly realize
other nation

s deserve
their same-

due as his
own blood-bred

still Napolean
ic death-find

s.


## Why trans

late a poem
isn't your

s the–closer–
it–become

s otherwise.


## Debussy' (4)

a) s quartet

(first move

ment) in
the sun-shine

shadowing
s of a minor

key.

*b) Piccolo-*

touching

s of fleet
ing (and

yet) less im
pulsing mo

ment
s.


*c) The free-find*

ing transpar

encies of that
slow movement

(though still)
longingly un

resolved.


*d) a final too-*

much–of–that

as a middle–
aged woman

intimate
ly overdress

ed.

## Schulhoff'

s 5 pieces
for string quartet

danced show-
pieces most–

successful
ly in-the-

swing-of-thing
s cunningly–

contrived.


## Beethoven'

s opus 132
slow movement

so richly-
depthed at

the altar of
an ever-pre

sent (yet dis
tantly self–

encompassing)
God.

*Beethoven'*

s late quartet
s so oft rhy

thmically-dia
loguing their

tensed-intrin
sic needs for

a source-in
volving theme-

sense.


*That night*

moonfully-
eclipsed its

in-describ
ing darkness

es.


*Can one*

successful
ly-word a

wordless
ly abstract-

music.

# *Brahms' 2<sup>nd</sup> String Quintet (3)*

*a) as an over*

ly weighted

treasure-
ship dulled-

down to its
irretriev

able sound-
depths.


*b) When the*

urge-for-song
drowned-out

its fully-bott
omed ground-

swells.


*c) dramatical*

ly (insistant
ly) overcoming

its classical
ly-sensed

transparen
cies.

## Mozart's K. 515 String Quintet

as cloud-shift
ing light-in

tervals of an
always-apparent

ly transpar
ent summer day.


## Mendelssohn's 2<sup>nd</sup> String Quintet

at times roman
tically over–

sensed (yet)
classical

ly (intimate
ly) sound-in

volving.


## Sunday-for-the-dead *(Totensonntag)*

also called
"Eternal Sun

day" as if the
dead are either

eternally that
or have simply

vacated their
timed-presence

for the ston
ed silent-re

verence of
those eternally

left-behind.


*End-of-the-church-year*

as if years
could end with

out going on
as a dead-end

ed street to
where it wasn'

t anymore
(or perhap

s) the end
of what was

(and is) invisib
ly continu

ing on.

# Mourning (2)

### a) Can one mourn

for a father

who achieved-
it-all and

(as Kafkas)
towering a

bove all that
littleness

of one's own
lesser accomp

lishment
s.


### b) Can one mourn

for a loving

mother who
would have i

maged him to
a shadowing

replica of
her always

higher-pedes
talled hus

band.

*Mendelssohn's St. Paul (Part 1)*

It could have
been the dra

matic/lyrical
unity of word

and sound that
left him 90

breathless
minutes of

holding-tight
hard-seated

to its al
most untouch

ably (time
lessly) there

ness.

## Part II

sweetly un
evened (as

the text) left
him (despite

those rousing
baroque/roman

tic choruses)
softly escounc

ed in the ease
of "he's done

it better than
this".


## It had alway

s been there
at an untouch

able distance
a porcelain

too-pretty-to
be-true paint

ed with color
s faintly re

mote from the
always of this

here-and now.

## *It snowed*

the night
through a

voiceless re
membrance

of what we'd
never really

known releas
ing a darkness

intensely
(yet still)

remotely
there.


## *It couldn't*

be blotted-out
now that it

had become
known as leave

s stained to
that very-bott

omness of au
tumn's dying-

out-reach.

## If there

had been a
moon that

night it
would have

been watch
ing-us-down

knowingly
bright per

sistant
ly-there.


## Shadowings (5)

*a) The ocean*

s never real
ly depth their

real-intent
but continu

ously wave-on
a soundful

(though sha
dowless

ly) repeat
ing al

ways indeciph
erable mess

age.

*b) If there*

had been an
unseen bird

flown through
the very-depth

of its alway
s-looming-

night releas
ing a voice

less shadow
colorless

ly remote.


*c) If he couldn'*

t sell his

always-remind
ing-shadow

he could at-
the-least

tame it as a
tiger mild-

eyed (though
still) domesti

cally in-wait
ing.

*d) A letter*

he'd never sent
but seemed-to-

have as felt-
through thought

s expressive
ly (though

still) unwritt
enly-there.


*e) He felt mo*

mentarily a
distant sense-

of-strange
ness as a

bird nameless
ly shadow

ing.

*Let us*

    start again
    (as we've al

    ways done)
    knowing-full-

    well this
    first lasting–

    snow freshly
    over-covering

    those over-
    drawn steps of

    ours.


*Winter*

    changes eye-
    forms depth

    ed to a cold
    ly inherent

    skied-blue.


*This cold*

    has reached
    a bottom-

    dwell of
    self-clutch

    ing secur
    ity.

## A ground-

touched harden
ed-snow

bird's sudden
ly-sensed

flight-in
stinct

s.


## Squirrel

ing acrobat
ics a branch

ed tight-
rope of leap-

climbing o
ther-side

whereness
es.


## Leaves

frozen-down
their last-

felt heart-
beat

s.

## I felt a

loneliness
for his be

coming island
ed middle in-

a-life-grasp
a lone reef

passioned
without a

self-continu
ing time-

cause.


## Shadowings

This snow-

tight winter
morning mess

aged only by
a lone bird'

s blackly
shadowing

response.

## The French

symbolist
s (not only

Rimbaud) left
me on-the-o

ther-side of
an evilly-pre

sent world
that can't

word-inhabit
me now.


## Reminding

of-Gatsby a
spacious

ly self-en
hancing

house room
ed with in

tently una
vailing-silen

ces.


## Her darkly-

leathered
hands press

ed tight-in
to the a

ging wrinkle
d-veins of a

faceless
ly unassum

ing smile.


## Across-the

way a window
ed-darkness

depthed space
lessly intent.


## Domenic

in Australia
under-water

ed the strange
ly-present

features of
free-float

ing fish as
if imaged

to his own
come-as-may

life-style.

*The snow'*

    s purifying
    light cleans

    ed even the
    time–holding

    depth of his
    most indwell

    ing thought
    s.


*A shadow*

    less winter
    morning that

    even careful
    ly contemplat

    ing words
    seemed as if

    echoless
    ly time–with

    holding.

## U. L.

most usual
ly adorned

in those con
trary multi-

colored
bottomed-

down self-as
sumption

s.

## A sudden

ly appear
ing bird

branched
his intuned

rhythmic
swaying a

most intimate
ly accustom

ed sensed-
arrival.

## This cold

seems so irre
pressive

ly-present
that it may

have taken
the warmth-

flesh out of
my self-

intuning
word-sense.


## His lecture

smiled to a
self-ironical

down-play
ing a theme

that failed
to inhabit

a grasp
ed-response.

## Out-leaf

ed branches
wintered

to a naked
loneliness

almost self–
compelling.


## For Rosemarie

morning
ed to the

flow-touch
of your tend

er hair's in
folding rhym

ed-attuning
s.


## Franz Beck symphonies

nervy-
pulsing

storm-and-
stress breath

ful interlude
s.

## Dreamed

on-the-run
being pursued

through the
night by an un

seen enemy
until it dawn

ed a Chirico-
like street

ever-distanc
ing through

his on-coming
fear

s.


## Händel's Messiah (6)

*a) so familiar*

ly voice-in

tuned that it
seemed to e

cho through
an almost

timeless re
membrance.

*b) Händel at*

his usual-best
as one so spon

taneously
there that one

never quest
ioned the ori

gin of his
(its) so-be

ing.


*c) His "Man of*

Sorrows" (how

ever repeated
ly invoked)

still seemed
vastly kingdom

ed beyond that
centrally pre-

establish
ing throne.

*d) Händel's*

counterpoint
(however celes

tially ascend
ing) still

seemed almost
as natural as

down-to-earth
every-day con

versation.


*e) The florid*

lines of High-

Baroque (e
ven those so

pompously
self-reassuring)

still seemed
as artificial

ly unkept o
ver-dressing

s.

*f) The repeated*

poetic-indul
gence of

"seemed"
here may be

a clue to
why Händel (how

ever deeply re
ligiously-in

volved) world
ly-Britished

its so appar
ent represent

ational nature.


*Lee the most*

critical
ly self-pro

tective person
I'd ever known

only twice
experien

ced crying
at the death-

bed's breaking-
off a long-dis

tant call.

*Those most cap*

able of defend
ing their own

self-interest
s are rarely

those most re
spectful of

the walled–in
barriers of

others possess
ed with e

qually valid
claims of–

their–own.


*The pearl*

ed–quality
of branch–

still(ed)
rain–drop

s.

# When he so

statuesque
ly appeared-

on-the-scene
I could almost

feel her curl-
up inside sweet

ened as a
pre-tasted

cookie just
waiting to be

crumbled-down to
his all-con

suming hand
s.

*Brecht's unfor*

> tunately-famed
> "love-poem"
>
> "Remembrance
> of Mary" isn't
>
> a love-poem
> at-all but
>
> a forget-poem
> of a relation
>
> only tempor
> arily his but
>
> hardly (as it
> would seem)
>
> theirs.


*Just before*

> this winter-
> tight dawn
>
> transform
> ing distance
>
> s of celest
> ial self-reveal
>
> ing quietude
> s.

## Advent

This night

depthed in
its own self–

overcoming
light–apprais

als.


## Haydn (3)

*a) Haydn's "Sur*

prise Symphony"

's successive
ly dance–light

currents of
time–transcend

ing gladness
es.

*b) Reevaluating Haydn*

Why should a
continual

ly first–time
freshness

realize only
a lesser low

er–level dist
inction well

belowed our
own so self–

indulgent
pathos.


*c) Did-you-hear*

(ever awaken
ed) to those

transparen
cies of light–

transcend
ing awareness

es.


*3ʳᵈ Piano Concerto (Bach, slow mvt.)*

as if that
other–world

of his silen
ced to our

own listen
ing-depthed

contemplat
ive renew

als.


## Mozart

and piano con
certo synonym

s for what'
s privately

(and most per
sonally) his

most self-re
vealing inti

macie
s.


## Advent-waiting (2)

*a) for what won'*

t happen ex

cept in that
receptive

silence momen
tarily tension

ed.

*b) Waiting as*

if it hadn'
t happened

before dis
tantly light–

embracing.

## Winter night' (4)

*a) s darkly invis*

ible hold as

if even time
itself had be

come irretriev
ably lost.

*b) Winter night'*

s the impene
trable source

of all those
unkept promise

s of our
s.

*c) Winter night'*

s sleeped–full
ness of all

those disen
chanting dream

s restless
ly unstill

ed.


*d) Winter night*

invisibly
looming a

bove and bey
ond whatever

unfathom
able conscious

ness.

# This wood (3)

*a) once clean*

ly-cut some

75 years ago
from the im

pending dark
ness of those

death-brood
ing times-of–

their
s.


*b) This wood*

death-stain
ed at its

dried-down
timeless

source.


*c) This wood*

now immovably
housed in a

love-guaran
tee of contin

uously protect
ive reassur

ances.

## Poems

must be no–
where–else

than inevit
ably–there.


## Dead voice

s now but in
escapable i

mages of a
timeless

past.


## "Its not nor

mal" his al
ways forward–

driven instin
ct as a hunter

dead–tracked–
scented.

## She needed

the softness
of soothing

phrases to
flesh her

tideful sea-
depth awaken

ings.

## When (2)

*a) When window*

s winter-time
that bare-

faced empti
ness.

*b) When these*

winter skies
seemed timed

even beyond
their open-

sensed contin
uitie

s.

*To read the*

Symbolist
s only in trans

lating a bridge
without the

fragrant tone
s of their

time-stepp
ed word-puls

ings.


*He didn't*

know where to
begin so it

began for him
as a wide

snow-felt
field open

ing-out to
the where

of a still un
folding be

ginning.

## Dream

> s that could
> n't tell-them
>
> selves-out
> to that a
>
> wakening mo
> ment of van
>
> ishing dark
> nesses.

## Open-ending

> s as a bare
> ly-touched
>
> through-cur
> tain to a
>
> where of
> never-having-
>
> been-there
> before.

## Cracow

> (near Auschwitz)
> those empty
>
> chairs of a
> public square
>
> symbolizing
> the dead-Jews

lost in the
dark of that

long-away
night.


## As night con

tinues to feel
much-the-same

as it alway
s-being-there

in its own
contemplat

ive silence
s.


## 2<sup>nd</sup> Choice

She always re
mained that

2<sup>nd</sup> choice in
habiting an

unchosen place
of his still

emptied dream
s.

*For Warren and Carol*

A small (now
nameless) vill

age somewhere
near the Austr

ian-Hungarian
border came

back-to-mind
mapped us in

to the midd
le of a no-

wheres-else.


*These Third-*

of-December

poems simply
wrote-them

selves-out
mostly una

ware of run
ning to a

still undiscov
ered (though

barely deciph
ered) end-

start.

# *Clarinet Quintet* *(Mozart 1ˢᵗ. mvt.) (3)*

*a) Soft shadow*

s melting in
to untouch

able wave
s.


*b) Slow mvt.*

as if time
had stopped

to a breath
less pause

of lightly-
densed remem

brance
s.


*c) The seduct*

ive voice of
the clarinet

poised through
those effus

ive stream
s of poetic

ally-sensed
cadence

s.

## *Clarinet Quintet* *(Brahms 1ˢᵗ mvt.) (3)*

a) *darkly-*

hued reflect

ively time–e
voking.


b) *At time*

s obscure
ly–voiced

as if tide
fully self–en

compassing.


c) *Adagio*

as if haunt
ed by time

less rhapsod
ically–impul

sed effusion
s.

*These hard-*

sensed winter
days frozen-

down to a time
less touch

less identity-
void.


*Brueghel'*

s "Winter
Games" child

ren–us to a
denial of

death's all–
consuming

bottomless
hierarchy.


*Now even*

these glass–
window

s eyed to
their in–sens

ed impenetra
ble death-

scope
s.

## This touch

ed–warmth
may flesh us

into those
purifying

streams of
lightful

invocation
s.


## Those (now)

transitory
rooms (mother

s) yearly Scars
daled us into

an intimacy
of distant

ly-kept time-
claim

s.

*All-those-*

friends-of-her
s left behind

to their age
lessly contem

lating death-
silence

s.


*Inge'*

s slowly los
ing her daily-

grasp of tim
ed-sequence

s.


*These winter*

ed trees thin
ned to their

scarcely-felt
shadowless

perspect
ives.

*Baudelaire'*

        s cat–poem
        (even not

        quite domesti
        cally situat

        ing) what
        can't be for

        eigned-there
        for-long.


*This so*

        closely–sensed
        winter night

        starred through
        the cold dis

        tances of its
        untouchab

        ly bright a
        wareness

        es.


*Dream*

        s flowing–
        through these

        vastly uninhab
        itable night–

        silence
        s.

## *"It all come*

s back to us
in-the-end"

(Strindberg)
as if judgement'

s (also) a
right-now sitt

ing-process
stooled high

above its time
lessly instinct

ive sense-
flow.


## *When some re*

lations become
so wordfully re

petitive of
their not-quite

self-revolving
time-sense.

## *A. B.*

so close-fist
ed tensed in

ner resolve
that not e

ven his small-
eyed glass-

fix could
reach far bey

ond a moment'
s refresh

ing breath.


## *Haydn or Beethoven's adagios*

"Saying the
most by using

the least"
as if the more-

of could lessen
the intent of

its always-in
herent there-

being.

## Light-on

> across-the-way
> limiting the
>
> scope of this
> overcoming
>
> darkness to
> but a momen
>
> tary-pause.


## Some made-up women

> What become
> s (in time)
>
> too over-culti
> vated as a
>
> garden routed
> to those self-
>
> same rows of
> their (once)
>
> so elusive
> ly pretti
>
> ness-display
> s.

## That habit

ual hunger–for–
word–growth

the very–depth
ed inter

ior chasms of
his own ag

ing–out
s.

## The diplo

macy of "a
measured re

sponse" may
also imply

the increas
ing need for

foot–and–in
ches ruler

s.

*They alway*

s did what
one should

Brought–up
their child

ren in the i
mage of their

own life–succ
ess But de

spite all
their loving–

efforts not–
one–of–them

turned–out
just–right.


*Those sharp-*

cutting wind
s snow–drift

ing the night'
s darkness

es right–down
to bottom

ed self–sus
taining sound

less vacanc
ies.

## Change-of-

tone change-of-
pace as if re

routed to a
somewhere

not yet vis
ually off–

sighted.


## A sudden

ly appear
ing bird

told–me–so
soundless

ly shadow
ing.


## For Rosemarie

whose still
thorough

ly enticing
body continue

s to land
scape my lin

gering desire
s to a suffi

ciently per
sistent depth

ed-cause.


## *Antonello da Messina (5)*

*a) "Madonna Benson"*

*(Washington)*

as if her
flesh had been

transform
ed into the

image of a
spiritual en

chantment.


*b) St. Sebastian (Dresden)*

as if Chirico'
s space-abstract

ion facially
self-illuminat

ing.

*c) Madonna and Child (Messina)*

Their unity
of face and

touch dress
ed to jewell

ed-length dark
nesses.


*d) Annunciation*

*(Palazzo Abatellis Sicily)*

Not even
Bellini could

beautify her
beyond such a

cloth-enclos
ing eye-flesh

ed mysterious
ness.


*e) Portrait of a man (Cefalù)*

I wouldn't
trust him with

an inch-more
of his cunn

ing-smile'
s ubiquitie

s.

## In-sight

　　　s light-glan
　　　ce sparking

　　　ly-resistant
　　　jewelled.


## If all are

　　　created–equal
　　　it's only be

　　　cause life and
　　　death fully in

　　　habit the leng
　　　th of our une

　　　qualled time-
　　　span.

## *"Blind following the blind"* (Breughel)

They kept-
close to that

same–certain
ed path hold

ing tight to
the rhythmi

cally forward-
pulse of the

other's e
qualled claim

s high–above
a depth to

their very
bottomed-

down self.


## *His life*

had become
a constant

pulling–her–
back from her

own distanc
ing ways as

if he could
retrieve but

a shadow
ing image of

his own di
minishing-

self.


## Over-depthed

The little-
length renew

ing runs of a
squirrel'

s sky-highed
over-depth

ed.


## I caught

that little
girl's sem

blance eye
s to a mo

mentar
ily here and

only-now.

## Getting-used

to that no-
answer respon

se as a time
less-void nak

edly-alone
d.


## Hyphens

are like
clothing-

tighter its
colorful in-

bound
s.


## Buds that

froze at
their very-

source dried-
in death-mo

thered.

*Cold and*

threaten
ing weather

too close to
feel-certain

in a time of
oft self-es

caping need
s.


*In this stati*

cally-apparent
cold even the

self-sufficient
roofed-down

houses seem
as if cut-

off from a
memorable

sense-of-
touch.

## Sleep-comfort

s the ease of
being pillow

ed in the im
measurable

depth of dream
ed–solitude

s.


## Frames *(for Charles and Lenore) (3)*

*a) Are frame*

s a final en
closing of

a picture'
s own touch

ed–complet
ion.


*b) Or are they*

meant to be
seen–through

to what's
still envis

ioned–alive.

*c) Or do they*

remain as an
enduring self–

finding a
painting's

increasing
ly over–reach

es.


*Why do*

tastes change
(even with

in ourselv
es) as if

time invisib
ly revolving

untold (though
still incon

clusive) appear
ances.

## Pulcinella *(Stravinsky)*

If the past

can be reviv
ed to live

again in the
colors and

tones of our
always-now

Then death
may have only

taken but a
momentary

respite.


## Romances op. 40 and 50 *(Beethoven)*

A Beethoven

neither classic
nor pre-modern

but one who
beautifie

s the life
that wasn't

his to become
most satisfy

ingly-now.

*Pinchas Zucker*

man "sounded
it just right"

as if each
tone had be

come phrased
and individual

ly personed
beyond the com

poser's most
intuitive

ly curtained–
intent.

*Those who*

feel "we think
and feel it

mostly alike"
either have

never shadow
ed their own

intangible
self-being

and/or have
mirrored the

image of o
thers through

their own
glassed uniden

tifiable-self.

*Why is it*

> that poetical
> ly-silenced
>
> Corot unspeak
> ably timed a
>
> bove my inher
> ently creative
>
> desk contin
> ues to frame
>
> me (and it)
> to the length
>
> and depth of
> its own time
>
> less quiet
> udes.

*If child*

    ren first see
    and feel that

    always–elusive
    depth of word

    less meaning
    s then lang

    uage (however
    artificial

    ly imbued) must
    rediscover

    that self–
    same source of

    its very-be
    ing.


*A fish depth*

    ed beyond the
    dark of its un

    told being
    but a remote

    image of why
    time still re

    mains invisib
    ly alert.

*Even as a*

    Christian

    I wouldn't
    deny the last

    ing beautie
    s of this

    world's still-
    reclaiming

    and most sensi
    tively self-

    fulfilling
    hold-on-us.


*Snow e*

    choes its own
    soundless

    voice beyond
    the night'

    s indwelling
    darkness

    es.

*Are there*

> still (as in
> Shakespeare'
>
> s time) por
> tents and vis
>
> ions that en
> lighten an
>
> always secret
> ly inbecoming
>
> future.

*Do we need*

> to be taught
> to understand
>
> or is learn
> ing only a
>
> means of re
> discover
>
> ing that oft
> muted and i
>
> solated other-
> side-of-self.

# Christmas Carols (5)

*a) "We three*

Kings of Orient
are" a time

less (even
spaceless)

heavenly
longing to a

distant ever–
present star–

calling.


*b) Adeste Fidelis*

a consuming
gathering–

in as of the
field's first

fruits that in
visible urge

beyond the
lure of our

own fleshly–
prompted

time–span.

*c) "Es kommt ein*

Schiff geladen"

Waiting on–
shore for the

pre-destined
arrival of

Him who shall
ease the ti

dal-swell of
our timeful

ly unfulfill
ed being.


*d) "O little*

town of Bethle
hem"'s dream

less sleep of
its star-guid

ing quietude
s.

*e) "Wie sollen wir*

Dich empfangen"

"How shall we
receive Thee"

helpless and
nakedly self-

revealing en
fant in the

dire loneli
ness of our

own so perish
ably inconceiv

able presen
ce.


*These bare-*

barren winter
days so tight

ly-sensed
that not e

ven the touch
of a flower

ing moment
could awaken

a reviving
life-pulse.

# Haydn's Creation (5)

*a) Is each instru*

ment (as the ani
mals describ

ed) a voice
individual

ly heard as
they're called–

out–of–the–
void to their

instinctual
life-presence.


*b) Haydn's*

"naïve" relig
ious world–

view yet so
familiar

ly ever–pre
sent as if

that yester
day could

once again in
habit this

God–forsaken
world–of–our

s.

*c) Händel's en*

compassing
strength

(though e
ver-present)

transform
ed into a

new-found
clarity of

lyrical ex
pressive

ness.


*d) Haydn'*

s "light" out
of that deep

ly-hued dark
ness of a

totally un
fathomed

world ever-the-
more radiant

ly bright.

*e) Strange-to-*

say(?) that
Haydn (so un

fortunately
married) could

so idealize
such a state

of his own
non-being.


## Looking to

see what one
hasn't before

as if sight
had become a

one-way hollow
ed emptiness

soundless
ly echoing.

*How can these*

motionless
ly dried–

down tree
s become sapp

ed again leaf
fully self–a

dorning pleas
ured.


*For Qian*

The world-of–
books however

tightly–paper
ed–and–bound

hers to a fu
ture lifeful

commitment.


*A room left*

behind with my
mother's death

windowed
from a sense–

of–place now
self–confin

ing.

## Only unremem

bered time empt

ied-bare e
ven from the

touch of lost
perspective

s.


## A poem

(however arti
culately con

ceived) re
mains as (per

haps) only an
insufficient

means of tim
ed-remembran

ce.


## For Rosemarie

Your timeless
beauty can

only fade
through my

eye's dimin
ishing light-

sense.

*An uninhabit*

> ed balcony-
> to-the-sea
>
> designed to
> perpetual
>
> rhythmic ac
> cords left
>
> lifeless
> ly wave-in
>
> tent.

*Those clean-*

> teeth manne
> quin smile
>
> d him in-to
> a dental appre
>
> ciation of
> beauty's singul
>
> ar artificial
> ly cleans
>
> ing-glow.

## Winter'

s stripped-
down tree

s left Pink
still naked

ly unrehears
ed for time'

s continual
ly impending

self-assuran
ces.


## A poem

that needed to-
be-said but

shouldn't
continued to

urge itself
as an untamed

beast that e
ven words

couldn't
finally paper-

down.

234

## Are most busi

ness–women dress
ed in the fabr

ic–colors of
their own self–

commitment
Or are these al

ternate way
s to a more-

expressive
articulate–

person.


## Music that

continues to
stay-with-us

voicing what
may seem

(at first)
an almost haunt

ing self–motif.

# Dead-sensed winter (3)

*a) timed to the*

certain-poise

of that sit-
down self-supp

osing black
bird.


*b) Dead-sensed*

*winter*

remotely star
red ever-beyond

the touch of
our voiced-

for presence.


*c) Dead-sensed*

*winter*

at the dawn
of its distant

ly ever-increas
ing light-in

stinct
s.

## Light-on

    across-the-
    way shadow

    curtains
    the impress

    ion of what'
    s become

    vaguely un
    known.


## Frozen leave

    s motionless
    ly dead-fathom

    ing a panto
    mine of lifed–

    forgetful
    ness.

## San Manuel Bueno

### Unamuno (3)

a) *couldn't*

quite silence

his resurrect
ing faith from

the persist
ing doubts of

an almost truly-
convincing

Christian
life-persuas

ion.


b) *His lake and*

mountain

ed-soul mirr
oring an al

most god-like
home-familiar

ity.

*c) Had that*

non-believing
martyr become

but a fake-im
itation of

his most-Cath
olic churche'

s spiritual
ly-dressed

façade
s.


## Madonna and Child
## (Lorenzo Monaco ca. 1420) (for Chung) (2)

*a) Your eyes*

speak un
seen word

s and un
spoken dis

tance
s you.


*b) How fine*

can the fab
ric of touch

self-reveal
ing.

## *What she*

dreamed (so
distantly un

real) became
place strange

ly pre-inhab
ited.


## *Jiménez in translation* (5)

*a) No where*

than only
that word–

sensed mean
ing.


*b) (and yet)*

too golden
to glow a

new its own
untarnish

ed self–right
s.

*c) 1898*

Is that "gold"
the last of

the lost colon
ies but faint

ly brighten
ing those o

ceans–away.


*d) As his Tagore*

romantical
ly suspect

Clichéd
right-down to

its indwell
ing feeling

fullness.


*e) (but oft)*

themed to
that existent

ially–real
"I/thou"

ness.

## Qian

There be

came a too-
much-at-

once about
her cultural

ly full-shopp
ing.


## Is Spanish

better attuned
to translat

ion-right
s (even the

poems) seem
ed in their

word-sense
as a through-

crossing
bridge self-

adapting.

## Catching-up

when that
path seemed

so used-down
scarcely

foot-marked
beginning

s.


## Some writer

s (as Unanumo)
seem so-many

placed Facing
even more than

those all-dir
ections-at-

once (at
times) face

lessly obscure
ed.


## Those sensual

ly-religious
always endanger

ed by that o
ver-growth

ed self.

*The cold*

> thrust of
> this threaten
>
> ing winter
> sky wind–
>
> through his
> shadowing
>
> irretrievab
> le self.

*A winter*

> stillness
> as if even
>
> the immovab
> le shadow
>
> s time-seclud
> ing.

*When Christ'*

s brought-down
to a daily

kind of broth
erly friendli

ness as if
His suffering

ran less blood-
deep than smil

ing-composur
es.


*The church'*

s brightly-
belled accom

paning its emp
tied pewed-

shadowing
s.


*Now even*

the psalm
s have become

flattened
of their al

ways word-en
compassing

presence.

*Still that*

           unanswer
           ing open-skied

           bird's one-
           tone song re

           solately
           branched.


*Victoria'*

           s "O Magnum My
           sterium" phras

           ed him into
           those darken

           ing abodes of
           still unre

           solving bright
           ness

           es.


*This river'*

           s dried-down
           tensely-

           stoned rhy
           thmic-inhabit

           ing
           s.

## First-time

friends (and
yet familiar

ly there) as
if we'd al

ways been
spaced to a

common-time-
sequence.


## Missionis

ing Jews had
become for

them (as it
may also have

always been)
a means of re

assuring their
own ever-tim

ed self-call
ings.

## *Piano Concerto 27* (*Mozart*) *(2)*

*a) Larghetto*

as if time
had been still

ed–down to
that most in

timate touch
of its own

self-aware
ness.


*b) Finale'*

s a classic
al way of

calling one
self back to

the bright
ness of life'

s always rhy
thmic self-o

vercoming
s.

## Christmas Concerto *(Corelli op. 6,8)*

a reserved-ser
ious intently-

controlled
way of reali

zing the deep
ly human-per

sonal message
of Christ's in

carnation.


## Can a small

chamber ensem
ble attain to

the fullness
of Mozart's sub

tlely shadow
ing transpar

encie
s.

## On Presents (4)

*a) Some indulge*

in the splend
or of giving

more than
their own per

sonal committ
ment.


*b) Others*

(more intent
on their own

personal pres
tige) find it

easier to give
than to re

ceive.


*c) Christmas*

should become
a special time

of answering
the fullness

of what Christ
has given

us.

*d) True to many*

children's
special need

of bringing-
up their own

parents I
(as a stud

ent) attemp
ted (with just

those rightly-
chosen book

s) to further
their much ne

glected educat
ional-endeav

ors.


## Has Christmas'

ornament
al-trimming

s replaced
those fulled-

up domicile
s forbidding

the poor Christ-
child's entran

ce.

251

## Those most

prone to mor
alize about o

thers often
try-to-con

ceal the full-
length of

their own
duly hung-up

Christmas-
stocking

s.


## Where the sad-ones sit

This is where
the sad-one

s sit buried
in the shadow

ing-depth of
their silent

ly remember
ed thought

s.

## Lorca'

s imagery
never seemed

to meet where
it began strange

ly foreign it
routed me to a

no-ways-back.


## For Rosemarie

Open curtain
s your light-

illuminat
ing face pre-

sun-timed in
tuitively-

sensed.

## Blue's not

always blue
a summer blue

and a winter
one imply a

different
depth-of-see

ing – blue
changes color

s while mood-
evoking.


## Lorca's

poems oft too-
striking a

cutely fail
to settle rest

fully-homed.


## Framed

Those pict
ures framed–

you to a time
that left me

uncertain
ly-where.

*He'd often*

smiled young
children in

to the softly-
timed me as

we of their
eye-length

ed exposure
s.


*Question-*

marks should
mark-out

what remain
s indistinct

ly-uncert
ain.


*Only the* (for Charles)

poem as a

finished
painting

can live a–
life-of-its–

own when it'
s securely

self-inhabit
ing.

## For Rosemarie

He instinct
ively realized

he could only
love-a-woman

who could
dream-him-

home.


## "The benefit of a doubt"

as if doubt
s could arti

culate any o
ther benefit

s than those
open-spaced

uncertaint
ies the pane-

glassed cen
ter of an un

fathomed mir
roring self.

# Callings (7)

*a) Snow-field*

s timeless
ly out–spread

ing the wind'
s perpetual

calling
s.


*b) The sound*

less voice
of night's se

cluded silen
ces.


*c) He sat self-*

surround
ing the vast

depth of un
told silenc

es.

*d) This voice*

less night'
s moon-inten

sing aware
ness.


*e) Where the*

wind's contin
uous flow

cloud-awaken
ing.


*f) Overcome*

with night'
s indwelling

calling
s.

*g) An unseen*

bird morning-
voiced its

coloring re
newals.


## Intuitively-sensed *(5)*

*a) He knew e*

ven before
he realiz

ed intuitive
ly-sensed.


*b) Plato and*

Maimonide
s so pure-

truthed deny
ing the un

harvested
realms of

those poeti
cally-entran

cing other-
world

s.

*c) The mind of*

the imaginat
ion as moon–

bright as
this night'

s unblemish
ed light-fo

cus.


*d) Beauty'*

s mysterious
ly darkly

veiled e
ven beyond

the reach of
the mind's

nakedly de
fining clarit

ies.


## *Sleepless*

nights as at–
sea waved–in

upending dark
nesses.

## A light

pastel winter
sky as if a

woman appear
ing child-

like innocent
ly than-she-

really is.


## A day lost

not noted-down
as if only pa

pered could
realize its

lasting-in
tent.


## The same

distant bird
s perched on

their own im
movable thought

s Sentinel
s of a time

less aware
ness.

## Darkened-

down window
s as if time

had become se
cretly enclos

ed there.


## Anxious

ly undecided
as if facing

two-direction
s at-once mo

mentarily
foot-stanc

ed.


## Each day re

petitively-
samed as a

mid-life lady's
(however dress

ed) less in
terior color

ings.

# Quick-poem

s more-here–
than-there

readily
self-assum

ing.

# Pain *(3)*

*a) When pain ex*

acts its own
time and place

sourced to a
pre-determin

ed no-wheres–
else.

*b) For Rosemarie*

If only your
placating

eyes could
soften the in

tensity of
this time-en

during pain.

*c) This pain*

wears the
darkly envel

oping realm
s of my sleep-

flow down to
the bottom-

ground of a
thread-bare

disenchant
ment.


## *Darknesses (4)*

*a) Darkest*

night of the
year enclos

ed in a depth-
softness of

light incom
ing time

s.

*b) Can one o*

verhear (e
ven the e

choing touch)
of these en

veloping
realms of

darkness.


*c) The darkly-*

lit peaceful
glow of the

Christmas
message and

of His death'
s star-intens

ing pain
s.


*d) as if night-*

itself had

slept within
the cushion

ed-depth of
its indwell

ing darkness
es.

# Rain (6)

*a) Rain'*

s more like
the repeat

ing sound
s of unans

wered quest
ions.


*b) Rain'*

s like listen
ing to the

voice of one'
s own most in

timate inner
darkness

es.


*c) Spring'*

s the time
for antici

pating the
rain's awaken

ing flower
ings.

*d) Night rain*

s as the whis
pering of

sleep-with
holding quiet

udes.


*e) Winter*

rains the
cold-feel

of barely-
touched in

terlude
s.


*f) Rain today*

brights tomorr
ow's uplift

ing creative-
impulse

s.

# Distances (5)

### a) Distance

s are more
a spaceful

sense-of-lone
liness.


### b) Distance

s are the
soundless

voices of o
pen winds

and emptied
field

s.


### c) Distance

s are the
poetic need

for just–
the-right–

word–sense.

*e) Distance*

s are always
s beyond the

seas of one'
s shoreless

longing
s.


# *A friendship*

without cer

tain common-
ground as a

ship without
port though

colored flag'
s high-fly

ing.


# *P. S.*

After their
partner died

for most a
post-script

ed life post-
work post-

health after-
timed.

# Looking-back *(2)*

*a) as if lands*

caping a

time–escap
ing past

those now
familiar

stops through
an alway

s oncoming–
beyond

ness.


*b) Looking-back*

as if those
steadied–

eyes of your
s could real

ize the inter
ior life–

streams of
his very-be

ing.

## Dreams *(5)*

*a) At the movie*

s seated to
an unknown

life-sequence
of his un

real (though
startingly)

realized.


*b) Where space*

less fear
s and time

less premoni
tions origin

their all-con
suming death-

source.

*c) When known*

persons and
self-assum

ing places
suddenly ap

pear as if
mysterious

ly transform
ed even be

yond their
apparent

self-compos
ure.


*d) Dreams*

as if all
those life-

masks star
ing naked

ly through
our self-dis

sembling
fears.

*A child-*

     like Mendels
     sohnian dream–

     world trans
     parently time–

     reawaken
     ing.


*"How could it come to this"* (2)

     *a) they asked*

     (mostly after
     wards)

     as if that
     "it" were a

     blinding
     pre-determin

     ing force
     Satanical

     ly self-im
     personed.

*b) Causes (how*

ever persist
ently there)

can't answer–
away why we

failed to
stand again

st that al
ways–increas

ing ground-
swell.


*Thaw (4)*

*a) when the*

timeless
frozen wood

s loosen
their death–

consuming
grasp.


*b) the light*

caressing

touch of
soft Flor

idian breeze
s.

*c) when your*

melting eye
s the ocean-

depths of all
these self-

mirror
ing instin

cts.


*d) Thawing*

those time-
accumulat

ing distan
ces between

them.


## When time

ran-out-on-
him as a

mountain
stream dried-

down from its
rock-bottom

thirst.

*Do we learn*

for or from
ourselve

s as a time–
renewing

source.


*After-sea*

sons the poet
ic instinct

ual time–e
luding phra

ses.


*Do names*

offer a certain–
clue to our

timeful ori
gins.

## "D. Ps"

"Displaced
persons" from

theirs or
ours mostly

death-evas
ive list-call

ings.


## The sub

dued dull-touch
of berry-time

now dried-down
to its wind-

escaping im
pression

s.

## Christmas Oratorio *(Bach) (3)*

*a) More-than-e*

ver the choral

s with their
depth of commun

al expression
ing that many–

levelled faith–
of-his (and

of mine) as
well.


*b) The individ*

ual instrument
s so careful

ly chosen to
match the son

orities of
those (at

times) over
long aria

s.

*c) All-of-what*

evers-to-be-ex
pressed here

The trumpets
brightful call

ings the inner
sweetness of

Mary's bedtime
child-caress

ings The contra
punctual strength

of those vast
choruses and

(even) the in
strumental

ease of depth-
lyrical phras

ings.


*He lost so*

much of him
self in such-

a-short-time
(wife and mo

ther) that
he seemed as

if (perhap
s) somewhat

open-spaced.

*Does all*

that light-glim
mer peaceful

longings of
pre-Christmas

time us to
a world more

real than we
could realize

why.


*Too-person*

al-poems may
im-person o

thers with a
rarely-shared

(though impli
citly felt)

sameness.


*Being "at-*

a-loss-for-
words" may

lesser-one-
down to its

expression
less void.

*Loss (for Chung) (5)*

    *a) Is it only*

    when we lose

    that we tru
    ly appreciate

    what isn't any
    more as if

    that loss
    itself had

    (only then)
    taken-on real

    flesh-and-
    blood.


    *b) When loss be*

    comes an un
    known distanc

    ing within
    our very-

    self.


    *c) Loss create*

    s a new sense
    of timeless

    ly open-sk
    ied.

*d) 24./25. 12.*

"Welt ging

verloren
Christ ist ge

boren" as if
He had re

birthed the
very death–

of–us.


*e) Loss awaken*

s a quietly
transpar

ent sense–of–
sadness.


## 24./25. 12. (5)

*a) It wasn't*

the apparent
snow but the

quietly sub
dued sense–of–

its consum
ing white

ness.

*b) 24./25.12.*

Rosemarie'

s Christmas
tree fresh

ly dressed
and lit out

of the growth
of its hand-

touched Christ-
purity.


*c) 24./25. 12.*

Only love

can near-us
to the my

stery of His
earth-trans

cending.

*d) 24./25. 12.*

A light o

therwise
than light

A love be
yond our-own

sensed eter
nal-flame

That always-
present un

touchable
truth.


*e) This day as*

if lifted
from the dawn

of its very
light-aware

ness.

## Some person

s are so self–
enclosed as

a book that
can only be

read while
consider

ing its bound–
in content

s.

## That un

seen bird
sang himself

out of the
darkness

to his own
sense of

light-color
ings.

## Lean-meat

a poem fired–
down from its

fat-filling
over-reach.

## Cold-harden

ing sap pulsed–

down that win
ter tree's

lessening
rhythmic–

flow.


## The dead *(their voiceless presence) (11)*

*a) Even if the*

dead are list
ening why

fear the un
told darkness

of their voice
less-presence.


*b) Do we re*

vere the dead
by not liv

ing the last
ing truth of

their alway
s–now.

*c) A belief*

in spirit
s may quest

ion the real-
substance of

our own self-
being.


*d) Last*

night I dream
ed her alive

though she
only answer

ed through
her voice

less–presen
ce.


*e) If all's*

still not said
(perhaps)

they realize
more of that

unanswer
ing truth.

*f) She became*

helpless
ly pre-voic

ed (as Cass
andra) with

that always–
impending

oncoming
death-route.


*g) "Ghost Trio"*

*(Beethoven)*

Did that

"Ghost Trio"
so–shortly in

habit Beethov
en's eerily–

pulsed phras
ings.


*h) "Ghost Sonata"*

*Strindberg*

(not quite e

venly balanc
ed in the

here-and-now)
"Ghost Sonata"

an ever–
threaten

ing beyond
ness.


*i) Thornton Wilder*

*("Our Town")*

(as a true
Christian)

realized the
hopeful sure

ty of a spir
itual never–

return.


# *If (as is*

said) some door
s close-be

hind while o
thers open-

out then life'
s a change

able process
to an unknown

though alway
s coming-on

through
ness.

## 25. 12.

A warmth
Christmas

day as if the
babe-Jesus

had also ta
ken-on for

us the desol
ate cold of

this all-pene
trating home

less world-of-
ours.


## Dreams (8)

*a) He knew he*

must get-there
not knowing

where or why
he became

lost in a
timeless

labyrinth.

*b) The climb*

continued e
ver-higher

no hold left
falling in

to a space
less void.


*c) She became*

as an inter
changeable

person dress
ed in such

varying color
s that e

ven the touch
of her could

expose yet a
nother voice

less person.


*d) A soft con*

tentment–
like feeling

almost like
a cloudless

transpar
ency.

*e) As a child*

swinging
the reach of

its thought
s ever-beyond

the evasive
touch of

windless-
sound.


*f) Clothed-*

tight Jewish-
starred in

that time
less train

so-feared
he became im

personal
ly-aware.


*g) Waiting for*

you to re
turn that

house empt
ied itself

out to a
spaceless

void.

*h) As a leaf*

ful frog
snake-scar

ed into its
total confine

ment.


## Can blood-

sourced relat
ions run-dry

even as the
light-intense

mountain
stream

s.


## The day-

after slow
s to its

own-sense
of timeless

ly-there.

## A *snow*

less winter
bare-ground

to its tight
ened wind–

calling va
cancie

s.


## *Do we grow-*

up to what
we've alway

s been as a
fruit ripen

ed to its
own pre-form

ing fullness
Or are the

roads (taken
or not) lead

ing us be
yond the very-

length of our
own once-be

inged.

## *A bee room-*

surprised
at its mid-

winter buzz
ing the en

circled possi
bilities of

its off-time
appearance

s.


## *Can we (also)*

realize a work-
of-art through

the sensibili
ties of other'

s word and
eye-touch.


## *Dialogued* (for S. L.)

He keyed him
self to the

vastly undis
covered ac

cords of his
piano's own

self-select
ive response.

*Wind-phas*

ing these
time's oncom

ing undiscov
ered possibil

ities.


*a) Phantom*

s of night
these darkly-

naked branch
es grasping

time's cer
tain hold-on-

us.


*b) These leaf*

less branch
es emptied

of all but
the wind's na

kedly repeat
ing unanswer

ed call.

*c) Bared-moment*

s as if only
inhabited

by perpet
ually desol

ate in–hold
ing silenc

es.


*Are the color*

ing–fabriced
dresses of

her most sel
ective moment

s but a mean
s of seclud

ing the depth
s of her se

cretly inter
ior–self.

## A warning a

gainst too
much too soon

overwhelm
ing those

still untouch
ed private

ly-securing
intimacie

s.


## If we could

only learn a
gain by listen

ing ourselve
s into those

voiceless
realms of seld

om-withhold
ing quietude

s.

## For Peter's 9ᵗʰ birthday

Quieting shad
ows silent

ly awake to
the intimac

ies of his
child-like i

magination.


## For Rosemarie (3)

*a) Rosemarie'*

s Christmas
tree fully-depth

ed the choice-
sense of her

most articul
ate light-fan

tasies.


*b) A winter*

morning's
cloud-respon

sive light-at
tunement

s.

*c) For Rosemarie*

when your
voice become

s soften
ed to its in

dwelling
light-blue

s.


*Smoke*

    dreamily a
    scending its

    slowly vanish
    ing cloud-

    sense.


*A psychother*

    apeutic smile
    protruding

    her always-
    most-concern

    ing cheek-
    spread.

## Alena at 12-plus

Too young
to be a wo

man too well-
formed for a

mere-child
She inhabited

a double-world
of puppet-

play and less-
ripened woman

ly-instinct
s.


## (After the Chinese)

Some friend
ships don't

quite even-
out as the

smooth ri
ver bank

s.

## Times a

drift as a
boat anchor

ed-free from
a shifting–

sandy bottom
less–deep.


## War pain

suffering
at such a

distance
from here

that they
seemed as if

remote
ly unreal

ized.

## An aging

love spring-
time pleasur

ed as tree
s rooted in

winter's cold-
down-depth

yet still e
ver-evasive

ly young.


## Poems from the Chinese
*(in memory Prof. Otto Ladstetter) (6)*

*a) When wine*

(at the last)

bottoms–down
the poet's still-

suspending
sensibilit

ies.


*b) When moon*

and trees mir
ror mood-in

voking re
flection

s.

*c) A faintly*

quieting sense
of untouch

able distanc
ings.


*d) Rivers bloss*

oming the
scent of col

oring full
nesses.


*e) A bird's*

song (however

brightly hue
d) instinct

ively shadow
ing.

*f) When cloud*

s withhold
ing those un

spoken time
s of distant

awakening
s.


## *Messiah* (Händel) (6)

*a) a self-con*

suming word-
sound energy-

plus.


*b) Even before*

we're ready
for-start

There as a
pre-appear

ing bird-
stance.

*c) When counter*

point counter
s any hesitant

chance-find –
non-stop

through
ways.


*d) A faith*

that's more
ground-swell

ed self-assur
ance.


*e) Reflect*

ive time-pau
ses his-own

momentary
depth-breath

ing.

*f) Why Haydn and*

Beethoven called
him "the greatest"

because Händel
thorough

ly convince
s more than

any composer
I've ever known

most-certain
ly himself!


## *Jane Eyre* (BBC film) (4)

*a) Jane's too*

good to be
really-so

too always-
righting a

moral/humane
example to

be thorough
ly convinc

ing.

*b) She's more*

a contrast–
character

to the super
ficial mode

s (and dress)
of her so–Vict

orian counter
parts.


*c) Rochester'*

s self–quest
ioning real

flesh–and–
blooded down–

the–middle di
viding blind

ed true–loved.


*d) An eerie oc*

cult–Gothic
watch–out–

for–ghosts
kind–of

seat–tighter
than time de

serves long–
breathed.

*Can one*

think-thing
s so intense

ly-true that
they actual

ly take-on
shape-and-

form.


*Death-blank*

image imperson
ally staring

an impenetra
ble (though

immanent
ly danger

ous) distanc
ing.


*When the*

moon's pond
reflect

ing a depth
of quietly-

waved time
lessness.

## Why (7)

### a) Bruckner

massive
ly depthed-

in the organ'
s impending

flow never
wrote a sin

gle tone for
its always

there-being.


### b) Why Haydn

self-fulfill
ing in God

ly praise
left that so

Christmas-
message un

toned.


### c) Why some

happy-ending
s leave us

with an in
completed

sense of
what's-more-

to-come.

*d) Why*

the most suf
fering of

all people
s still re

main so opti
mistically

self–intuned.


*e) Why*

The Lord re
mained so si

lently aware
of Israel'

s burnt-flesh
sacrifice.


*f) Why as the*

heavens re
vealed their

first uplift
ing light

these hous
es still

remained
chosen–down

in a self–
lingering

darkness.

*g) Why did*

some birds
remain in

their dark
and tightly

self-enclos
ing winter

habitat.


## Year's end *(8)*

*a) (and yet)*

more of the

same-time'
s self-be

coming.


*b) A new year*

dressed as
an uncertain

young lady
in cloud–

light expect
ant-response.

*c) At the end*

of an always–
beginning

as a statue
samed to a

direction
less there–

being.


*d) Why remember*

when it will
continue to

remember
you Dreamed

in a time
less there–a

bouts.


*e) Lost wife and*

mother to a
personless

void Why cele
brate that

lesser–sense
of an alway

s–becoming.

313

*f) A continu*

ally aging

New Year
but still hold

ing-tight as
that distant

bird branch
ed to a cer

tain-hold of
self-being.


*g) (and yet)*

time's continu
ally moving-

on as those
wind-evoking

clouds to an
always pre-de

termining
end-close.


*h) New Year'*

s faith in

a time-creat
ing uncreat

ed God my
master-of-

mind-and-mat
ter.

*Largo* *(Haydn Violin*
*and Cembalo Concerto, 1756)*

> even then
> a hesitant
>
> sound-evoking
> spaced-bare
>
> ness-through.

*Violin Concerto 4* *(Haydn)*

> Reheard (as
> if for the
>
> first-time')
> s language
>
> only his in
> tervalled
>
> thought-se
> quences inter
>
> acting
> s.

*Genuine'*

> s a trade-
> mark of naked
>
> ly mirror
> ing oneself
>
> first-through.

## January 1

Now that it
had arrived

time situat
ed itself as

an errant
bird motion

lessly self–
satisfied.


## Left-behind Scarsdale-Poems *(4)*

*a) That middle-of-*

the-town-of-Scars
dale park at

the center of
where sitting'

s become such
an easy–down.


*b) Off-sides*

where those
trees search

ing even high
er than his

mind's unlim
iting reach.

*c) March-color (after Ives)*

ing flag-par
ade left him

patriotic
ally side-lin

ed.


*d) (after E. M. Forster)*

More-than-any

thing-else that
wide room with

the light-en
compassing

view.


## Those Chin

ese mood-sen
sed poems i

magining
a unity of

touched-
light enclos

ures.

## Two-placed

persons as a
school-child

and that o
ther-face of

homed-escap
ings.

## Skiing

those facial
slopes of

down-sensed i
magining

s.

## Chinese

exile-theme
s as if that

distanc
ing from home

had become
poetical

ly self-trans
forming.

*A snow*

> that didn't
> come still land
>
> scaping his
> always-expect
>
> ant mood-silen
> ces.

*Reading*

> oneself into
> other person
>
> s leaves them
> as untouched
>
> as those out
> side "time-re
>
> claiming" stat
> ues.

*"Anything you*
*can do I can it better"*

> an ever-bett
> er means of
>
> dead-ending
> commonly-ex
>
> pressing
> friendship
>
> s.

## Poetizing

had become
(for him)

not only a
daily lyri

cal self-ex
pressive

ness but (al
so) an histori

cally-adept
chronic of

more than
facts-and-fig

ures could
possibly ade

quately reveal.

## Tirso de Molina

(as many Spaniard
s of his day)

Monk-like in
outer-disposition

but possessed
with an excess

ively explicit
Don-Juan imagina

tion that un
dressed even-more

than his self-
inhibiting

life-style.

## It was said

of Tirso that
he understood

woman to the
very-depth

of their own
inner-reach

es because
(as a monk)

he daily heard
their confess

ionally-time
less God-e

voking plead
ings.


## Still life

s stilled his
very-being

to a space
ful light-e

voking contem
plation.

## An early-morn

ing stillness
prevading this

room with an
unspoken

sense of si
lent expectat

ion.


## Light morn

ing winds breath-
touched those fa

ding (though
scarcely-felt)

realms of time
less remembran

ces.


## This dis

tant scent-of-
smoke evok

ing autumn
al light-trans

parencie
s.

## Searching

for a lost
key opening

those untold
rooms of an

elusive
ly unrealiz

ing past.


## Babi-Yar

The blood–

earthed bottom
ness of those

past–resound
ing mass–shoot

ings.


## Those dark-

sides–of–self
inhabiting

speechless
caverns of

vastly encom
passing fear

ed–echoing
s.

## Mozart's K 136 *(Symphony andante)*

so youthful
ly innocent

freshly trans
parent as if

spring had
just–bloom

ed its first–
time promise

s.


## Haydn's

little-known
62nd Symphony

as unexpect
edly appar

ent as if
just–birth

ed out of its
pre–forming

most–pleasur
able surpris

es.

# Rows-of-book

s mirroring
his back-mind

ed glance(d)
through page

s of unspoken
thought–felt

self–becoming
s.


# Roomed-

in attentive–
pages of (as

yet) untouch
ed poemed–si

lence
s.

## The why

question
ed him so

oft until its
emptied call

ings merged
into wave

s of the sea'
s intuned ex

pressive
ness.


## That un

expected claw
ed-like beetle

sat remote
ly self-content

edly poised upon
its cloth-fabr

iced most cer
tainly self-

reclining in
stinct

s.

## A slight

shift-of-light
momentarily

unspaced his
contemplat

ive mind-
sense.


## The way

that young pian
ist leaned his

finger's re
sponse into

the unspoken
depth of the

piano's resound
ing self-ap

peals.


## How my

Rosemarie re
mained so in

nocently
housed in a

world of post-
Schnitzler

ian play-on
types.

## A new-age

Germany econom
ically robust

soccered to-the-
full of its

(once again)
self-satisfy

ing leader of
an (almost) thor

oughly survived
post-war trau

ma.


## House on the Water *(Seehaus 1917)*

His name-
sake's a dream-

like impress
ion of an al

most poetic ser
enity.

## Modigliani'

s repetit
ive form

s seem al
most shaped

through the
invisible

eye of his
own self–

being.


## Morning

birds continu
ally circling

the height
of a vastly un

known cause.


## Transforming (2)

*a) Was the tempt*

ing untouched
beauty of Eve'

s naked-being
that fruit it

self seductive
ly transform

ing.

*b) The transform*

ing intimacy
of a quartet

stringed to
a phrased

harmonic-u
nity of per

soned-place.


## Blood be *(2)*

*a) came the her*

oic source of

Spain's unify
ing pride –

pure blood as
unjewish as

Hitler's Ary
an-cult.

*b) The Inquisit*

ion and bull–
fighting be

came the in
delible symbol

s of Spain'
s doctrinal

blood–purify
ing heroical

ly–masculine
self–identity.


## *Eine Kleine Nachtmusik* (Mozart)

(so much a
part of my

musical very–
being) that

it simply flow
ed–away its

own lyrical
ly–evolving

self–enchant
ments.

*Mendelssohn'*

s 2<sup>nd</sup> Piano Concerto

(more fingered
than spirit)

close-sensed
a romantic

stream of (an
almost) self–

inhibiting
conscious

ness.


*The Greek pian*

ist (German-
trained) to

such a concen
trated aware

ness as if
that express

ively-alive
piano must be

come contin
ually held–

back from his
own running–

off finger
ing-stream

s.

## That back-o

peration
lumbered his

free-finding
landscaping

s to an al
most sputter

ing stacco
ed half-

sense.


## Li Shangyin *(813–858) (4)*

*a) A change-of-*

sense poet
mood image

The idea oft
self-trans

forming.


*b) So modern*

I could al
most hear my

own voice-
stream's e

choing.

*c) Untitled*

while these
poems oft

deny their
own identity–

route.


*d) A linger*

ing sadness
vacantly

self–seek
ing.


## *Drift*

ing as wave
s upon the

vastness
of this o

cean's immea
surable

depth.

*When the an*

chor's uplift
ing his heart

from the bott
om-ground'

s securing-
hold.


*Spring*

winds a light
ness freed

from all–
that indwell

ing–sadness.


*The bright*

ness of this
moon's magnet

ic–force time–
searching.


336

## Wind

s whisper
ing tropical–

silence
s.

## Over

night the
ship changed–

course compass
ed to an un

certain un
known route.

## When his a

ging skin slow
ly began to

crack–open
the snake's

nakedly self–
emerging

form.

## Mozartean

His unfinish
ed poems lost-

at-sea from
their never-re

trieving
sound-sense.


## Women ever-

so finely
dressed in Mo

zart and Monet'
s lyrical-

transpar
encie

s.


## This morn

ing as if
called-out of

the night'
s ever-re

leasing dark
ness

es.

# *Emperor Li Yu'* *(3)*

*a) s poems of ex*

ile adrift

as water-li
lie's home

wards color
ings.


*b) Emperor*

Li Yu's
luxurious

loss golden-
traced shoe

s timeful
ly closet

ed.


*c) An empire*

lost 45 time
less poem

s retriev
ing unspoken-

silence
s.

## She became

so much an i
mage of her

own willful-
self that in

time she be
gan to mirror

but a face
less appear

ance.


## At the Airport (4)

### a) Horizon

ed distance
s beyond this

flat–plain
view–clouds–

immensing.


### b) Unfamiliar

travel–bound
faces moving–

on express
ionless.

*c) Dialogued*

his hand-
held book'

s balanc
ed-reading

himself
back.


*d) Window*

ed-view eye
spacing what

timeless
ly-seems.


## "Landing-

rights" the
plane smooth-

surfacing
his oft uneven

ed through-
telling

thought
s.

*Under-tongu*

> ed what's
> often thought
>
> though not-to-
> be-said tense
>
> ly-unabiding.


*Those fateful years*

> Can one un–
>
> past what's
> still earthed
>
> to their blood–
> down unremem
>
> ered depths.


*Reading Alice Munro*

> at times seem
> ingly petty
>
> ordinary
> yet wholesome
>
> and a touch
> of something–
>
> more original
> even–acute.

## For Chris

I took him in
to poetic–cust

ody – no–way–
out except a com

pleted fulfill
ing thereness.


## Not-the-u

sual–way no
aging–waiting

mother at the
door not that

touching home–
feel(ing) estran

ged That always
s windowed–

view of hill
s surrounding

encompass
ing not-the–

usual–way.

*Sleepy*

stop-over
s recycling

time's dark
ly-secluding

quietude
s.


*Her tempt*

ing smile(d)
him into

those ominous
under-current

s of surpress
ed-desiring

s.


*Beauty'*

s as self-de
scriptive

as the shift
ing tonalit

ies of Schub
ert's elusive

ly melodic
time-flow.

## Poems from Florida

It's difficult
not to soften

the language
when he's re

clining in the
persuasive

ease of cloud–
sensed dream–

sequence
s.


## His shaved-

off smile left
him premature

ly skull–
tighten

ing.


## These wavy

palms branch
ed impression

ed light–time'
s restful

contentment.

## Little girl

s shadowing
the assuming

heights of
their father'

s towering
remoteful

ness.


## Florida

times–itself
to the tidal

alternat
ing depth–

lengthed
ebb–and–flow.


## Heavy-stepp

ed domesticat
ing dogs time-

slowed to their
accumulating

age–sense.

*Denials* (2)

a) *I can't cele*

brate as Ives
America's

flag-waving
vividly color

ing a patriot
ically-intuned

holiday-spir
it.


b) *Walt Whitman*

left me sing
ing off-key

mass-forsaken
harmonies

language
indescribab

ly flat-tone-
d.

## Left-over

s as unanswer
ed asides

or imaging
dangling-pre

position
s vacantly

air-forsak
en.


## Was Hamlet'

s "method-to-
his-madness"

more like a
lesser-keyed

King David's
life-saving

opportune
blind-folding

his dumb-found
ed enemies

suspicion
s.

*Is the mater*

> nal instinct
> wombed in an
>
> all-encompass
> ing body and
>
> soul rhyme
> lessly possess
>
> ive as well.

*High-blown*

> winds from the
> north cloud-
>
> swelling in
> stinctual
>
> ly feared-
> premonition
>
> s.

*Storm-warn*

> ings these
> white wind-
>
> sensed gull
> s hastily a
>
> bandoning
> their fleet
>
> ing shadow
> s behind.

## Emptied

beaches only
the lone sand

s stretching-
out miles bey

ond the unknown
source of their

primieval be
ginning

s.


## Footstep

s in sand
washed away

with the mem
ories of their

tentative
ly time-touch

ing appear
ances.

## These recur

ring waves
rhymed in

to the sus
taining accord

s of the o
cean's vast

distance
s.

## Dying *(2)*

*a) the distant*

stars out as

but a faint-
glimmering

hope.

*b) He sweat*

ed-down those
impersoning

sheets dis
pairing e

ven of their
light-sensed

closeness
es.

## This soli

tary beach walk
ing his shad

owing fear
s at least

two-apparent
ly-closing-

in-steps be
hind.


## Time-sharing

Same room

same time-of-
year as the

same music
heard (and

yet) ever-so-
slightly

changed (as
he himself)

but a year
later.

## Betterments

they called
those cost–ap

parent artifi
cial bric–a–

bracs that se
lected our

room into
the special

fineries
of their up–

to–date(d)
taste–rout

ines.


## Martin K.

Swabian minis
terial–type

who wanted to
hear more of

those most in
timate and re

vealing detail
s more than

he really
needed–to.

## Sensing the

impact-of-word
s is like

feeling-out
the printed

design of
footstep

s tensely-e
choing.

## Some per

sons anony
mously star

ing-out as
statues be

yond their
mostly imper

sonal sense-
of-loss.

## Alice Munro'

s usual off-
hand easy-sway

of everyday
things in a

not-so-very-
easy sort-of-

way.

# My childhood (4)

*a) friend Robert*

more-than-any

thing-else
wanted a litt

le girl marr
ied to some-

one-or-other
to become

that (as yet)
unborn child.


*b) Robert*

smilingly-
loved some

what obese
scatter-

brained fun
ny semi-old

women – he
must have marr

ied one for-
sure.

*c) His favorite*

(and perhaps
only book)

Winnie-the-
Pooh he must

have reread
backwards-

forwards (and
perhaps even)

inside-out as-
well.


*d) He spoke*

the unspoken
language of

grasses flow
ers and tree

s who answer
ed-him-back

in-a-way
only he could

instinctive
ly decipher.

## Dreamed-fears (5)

a) *I heard the*

sounds on the

steps couldn'
t envision

that invisi
ble person

climbing the
upper stair

s of my most–
hidden ghost–

like–fear
s.


b) *A moonless*

almost unappar
ent night

only the faint
ly distant

cries of wild
creature'

s blood–end
ed.

*c) A white-gown*

ed faceless
woman across-

the-way call
ing in an un

known tongue
strange-to-

touch sound
lessly echoi

ngs.


*d) Those six-*

smiles-ougamb
ling ship's

alluring
lights rout

ed to their
incoming shore

lessly darken
ing depth

s.


*e) Night-shad*

ows on-the-
wall imaging

a scarce
ly decipher

able sound-
flow.

## Borderline

with such in
sinuating

suspicion
s she under–

fleshed her in
nocent victim

s from their
own core-true

upstanding
rightful

ness.


## Sleepless

nights as if
the depth of

dream–flow
had remained

but perpetual
ly surfaced.

## Did Mozart

die having ex
hausted the

perpetual
life-stream

of his creat

ive-instinct

ual pulse-
source.


## For Warren

If really
good poetry

can't trans
late its

sourced-unit
ies of word-

sense Why ex
tend bridge

s beyond
their out-wa

tering sound-
flow.

## It gradual

ly dawned-on-
him the sub

dued bright
ness of that

but half-spok
en morning

ed-sense.


## Genuine

(authentic)
is when word

s-themselve
s define a

no-other-place
than that act

ually-their
s.


## He though

thorough
ly reliable

and really too-
nice than to be

come other
wise than a

usually-there.

## Palms *(after Alice Munro)*

so expressive
ly wind–sensed

as a young
girl–ladie'

s first–time
kissed–down

to that inno
cently un

dressed state–
of–appearance.


## For Rosemarie

who fashion
s me younger

each day
through her

calmly content
ed self–repos

ing smile.


## These night

s always seem
darkly–longer

uneasing our
daily–releas

ed light–ac
cords.

*Tide out-*

> going that
> soft-sand–
>
> feel of in
> dwelling
>
> through-spo
> ken distanc
>
> ings.

*Egret'*

> s slender–
> white sleek
>
> ly-lengthed
> scarcely–
>
> touched se
> curing
>
> s.

*This beach*

> particular
> ly shelled
>
> with the fra
> mentary remain
>
> s of once
> self-seclud
>
> ing silence
> s.

## Grass-thick

ets inhabit
ing poison–

eyed snake–
illusion

s.


## Familiar

pole–sitter
s as those

old–fashion
ed Southern

rocking–chair
ladies most

ly time–elud
ing.

## So close

ly paired in
taste and in

that most in
timate realm

of personal
sensibility

(and yet)
there still re

mained those un
touchable

never-to-be-
crossed line

s of a quite
in-bred dispar

ity.


## For Rosemarie

Some women
must be re-seen

to ensure that
most intangi

ble realm of
an almost in

describably
encompass

ing-beauty.

# George

as helpless
as myself

in some most
ly personal

ways but dri
ven by an un

quenchable
creative –

need to express
what had be

come more an
intrinsic

part of his–
own–person

than eat
sleep and such

daily necess
ary require

ments.

*Even the*

      most hermet
      ic of person

      s can't re
      main exclus

      ively self-en
      dowed They

      daily dialogue
      their most

      question
      able person bey

      ond its own
      shadowing

      self-recept
      ivity.

## Answering George

That most
natural flow of

word-sound sen
sibilitie

s realizes
its own-source

But those most
intricately

thought-expos
ing poems a

totally re
flective part

of one's own
educative-

being.


## One can

only remain
friends with

one-self when
others become

encircled in
that-same i

dentity-
cause.

## When Beethoven

broke-out of
that classical

ly self-enclos
ing form-sense

he became as
isolated as

the early-Haydn
in an empti

ness of that
where-to-source-

sense a contin
uing self-com

pletion.


## Dawn

slowly warm
ing-out over-

the-beach
spreading its

touch-consum
ing depth.

# Dolphin

s sloping the
water's sur

facing depth
with an al

most poetic
phrase-find

ing.


# She must

have been a
round 50 when

she lost-her-
looks It was

for her (a
beauty by

birth) like
discover

ing a new per
son mirror

ing an estrang
ed looking-

back of a some
one-else.

## That ever-pre

sent Floridian-
moon enlarg

ing the depth
of night's

self-encompass
ing silence

s.


## All these

steps-in-sand
seemed so

criss-cross
ed like a

chaos-of-
gulls that e

ven the still
untouched

sands seemed-
like a haven

of no-wheres-
but-now.

*When word*

s blacken-out
not a sylla

ble left
only the dark

inertia of
that blank-si

lence.


*Hidden-trea*

sure sound-wav
ed at the ti

dal depth of
that lone a

bandoned o
cean.


*She became*

so-used to
thinking of

others first
that one wonder

ed if she hadn'
t become as a

disembodied
spirit.

*"Owl-moon"*

as if that
night had be

come haunted
with its in

tensely-claw
ed ghost-

like presen
ce.


*His night-*

darkened win
dow closed-

shut to the
sea's persist

ent calling
s.


*That poign*

antly-sensed
lean-down tree

dying the full-
length of its

time-consum
ing days.

## Mine are

the days whitt
led–down as

wood to where
there's noth

ing left
but word.


## For Louise Glück

such beauty in
a consisten

cy of reflect
ive–tone

sounds samed as
an equalled–

person time–
supposing.


## The apple

trees full–with–
a–fruit that

desired noth
ing more than

being cleans
ed–down from

their emptied–
thirst.

*I want to*

> look-the-way
> Rosemarie-
>
> sees-me with
> those compell
>
> ing (though
> soothing) eye
>
> s-of-hers.


*When word*

> s don't match
> their inher
>
> ent-sense
> like giving–
>
> birth to weed
> ed-flower
>
> ings.


*She's alway*

> s there a
> cross-the-way
>
> a haunted
> ghost-like
>
> apparent-
> statue.

## *Aunt Gertie*

preconceived
with a heavy-

weighted bossi
ness left her

mildly fluent
husband with

nothing but a
self-effacing

humour to
slip-out from

her permanent
ly stolid-

hold.


## *Tom*

a Vietnam-
veteran ex

posed not-e
ven-a-touch

of the resid
ual-hardness

in his open-
hearted com

posure.

*Their house*

> of-open-room
> s spacing a
>
> depth of time
> ful shadow
>
> ings.

*These shore-*

> eluding low-
> tide smooth
>
> nesses of e
> ven-sensed
>
> contemplat
> ions.

*Early-morn*

> ing swimmer e
> asing the
>
> weight of
> night's pre-
>
> assuming dark
> nesses.

## In these hes

itant winds-be
fore-dawn white

gulls gather
ing a diverse

sense of comm
unal together

ness.


## Are bright

ly-colored
patterned

dresses a co
vert mean

s of conceal
ing nakedly-

suggestive
desiring

s.

*Second-*

        thoughts still
        lingering

        unresolved
        moments of un

        answering
        question

        s.


*Did you*

        meet–his–his
        tory full–

        face or only
        that self-de

        ceptive smil
        ing now–

        time.

## For Louise Glück

I take less
er risks

the sole im
pact of crush

ed-snow Your
s the wider-

view at time
s flawed by

its contin
uously-sens

ed entour
age.


## Appreciate

how the snake
instinctive

ly knows how-
to-change

skins reveal
ing time-in

stinct
s.

## We never

asked more than
his simply-be

ing-there as
we both need

ed nothing o
ther than his

not unravell
ing secret

hide-out
s.


## Those women

who need-be so
wholely admired

can off-track
men from a

false-sense
of safe-se

curity.

## An unfulfill

ed person is
like a house

with an open
ed-door and

the bareness
of its still

emptied room
s.


## Some friend

s more diffi
cult to be ta

ken-alone
than with their

personed-com
plementary

wife's ever
self-assuming

presence.

## Beauty en

tices that
more-of-us

than even the
unknown out

lines of her
personed-

self.


## Some-thing

s remain never-
discussed as

her father
hidden-behind

his ever-pre
sent morning-

paper.


## For Corinne

Robert Frost'
s under-tongued

time-recurr
ing wisdom set

s place and
tone most al

ways self-con
taining.

## Some bird

s so tiny
they scarce

ly leave
marks-in-sand

just fly fea
thering-

light.


## Double-talk (2)

*a) Grandpa Barney*

behind closed-
doors opened-

out the intima
cies for his

innocent grand-
daughters to

protect again
st those besieg

ing instinct
s of errant-

young-men.

*b) Those errant-*

young men

(his grandson
s) were engag

ed in the al
ternate tactic

s of breach
ing those al

ways protect
ively–walled

skirt–hold
s.


*Horse-shoe'*

s familiar
dull–metall

ic sound-
sinking pre

viously unre
vealing

instinct
s.

## The pelican

just float
ing-on-air

as if time
had become

nothing more
than the ease

of the alway
s-present.

## H. B.

One doesn't
know where to

start with her
remains after

years of semi-
confidence

still landscap
ed in strange

hardly per
ceivable place

s.

*She looked*

harder-kept
as if time

had become
too-pulled-

tight for her
getting-out-

from.


*If money'*

s the-name-of-
the-game then

their souls have
become paper-

weighted.


*The Southern*

Civil-War and
that of The

North still a
fictive nation

enslaved in
their own histor

ical myth
s.

## If they'

re 3 Greek word
s for love

We'll need many-
more than those

to overcome
the last resi

dues of what
has become

rightly-call
ed "original

sin".


## Some learn

their psychol
ogy from the e

ver-changing
learned fash

ions Others
from the time

less insight
s of creative

writers But
those-most-adept

for life are
those who life-

it-live.

## Those American

s who deny

the founding
greatness of

Columbus' un
expected dis

coveries pois
ed at an un

historical
height of out-

timed self-super
iority.


## Time-sharing

Is time-shar
ing more a

sharing-of-
time between

your active-
life then and

your retired-
one here-and-

now Or a shar
ing more of a

disguised blend
ing of an ever-

present alway
s-you.

## Alice Munro

finally dead–
ended me

when her per
ceptive in

sights and
carefully–

chosen langu
age reached

those bottom
ed–stairs of

every–day tri
viality.


## Those up

ward straight-
lined apartment

lights seem
ed as if lift

ing sea-call
ed wave-ensu

ing boats a
shore.

*Perhap*

s few realize
what we criti

cize in other
s reflecting

our self-same
interior-

source.


*The truly*

poetic seek
s its own

self-reclaim
ing voice.


*Drifting*

shadows as
leaves wind-

swept past
their time-en

suring claim
s.

*Dürer'*

s most arrest
ing portrait

s penetrating
even–deeper

than flesh
and bone

could possib
ly reveal.


*Screened-*

in chairs
staring

through
night–

timed self-se
clusion

s.


*Cold-front*

emptying the
Floridian

beaches to
lonely stret

ches of sand–
bared imaginat

ion.

## Self-Portrait at 76

Lonely palm
at a poetic

height of a
wind–elevat

ing untouch
able reconcil

iation.


## Tiny wind-

daring black
birds denying

the impend
ing–colors of

a brightly-de
signed satiat

ed summer
day.


## For Chung

Are those early–
romantic trans

parent sadness
es somehow a

kin to the sen
sibility of A

siatic dream–
flows.

# *A nation (2)*

*a) that left its*

(perhaps) best

poet E. D. and
its (perhap

s) finest novel
ist H. M. in

self-isolating
obscurity

should have
questioned

long-ago its
own self-enhanc

ing superior
ity.

## Answering Charles Krauthammer

An evened-
tensioned

political
stability

may enhance
the necessary

claims for a
cultured soc

iety but when
it becomes an

end-in-itself
that garden of

flowering hope
s may wither-

down to its own
self-encompass

ing death-
route

s.

## Asking George the philosophic-scientist

If an "ungroup
er" can evolve

into an ob
scurely unknown

fish Why can't
french-fries

simply reappear
as reinstated

potato-chip
s.


## If that

"ungrouper"
isn't what

it's supposed–
to-be have

we all become
more-of-less

"ungroupers"
ourselves.

## Card-playing

T. V. and the
like as if

life wasn't
precious e

nough to be
spent-out on

artificial
time-waster

s.


## The German dilemma

It isn't diffi
cult to for

get especial
ly if you

haven't exper
ienced But

what will the
innocent-dead

say-to-that.

## Identity poems (6)

*a) If we're all*

in a process

of self-becom
ing Where's that

one-and-all
substantial

identity-per
son.


*b) Some image*

s absorb in
to our inter

ior-being no–
wheres-else

than that re
membered-

self.


*c) When the*

sea's horizon
disappear

s into that
other-side-of

our own unex
plored self–

being.

*d) Is the dark*

side of the
moon only

visible when
we've brighten

ed into its
always sense–

of-being.


*e) Why our kalei*

doscopic person
always remain

s a rediscover
ing wholeness

as each friend
realizes only

his special–
choice of our

adept very-be
ing.

*f) Pink topped-*

in his Sunday-
best waved

good-bye to
those lesser

days of his
ordinary

clothed-in
smile

s.


## Four for the

musical trans
parent-ideal

of the string
quartet But

also two har
monized couple

s circling an
ever-present

oneness of
their-own

self-certain
ing sufficien

cies.

*The composed-*

> sureness of the
> masterful blue
>
> heron statured
> at sunset the
>
> ever–permanen
> cy of its own
>
> truly authent
> ic self–creat
>
> ive being.

*Dawn awaken*

> ing this dark
> ened room
>
> to a fluency
> of its slow
>
> ly formed–a
> wareness
>
> es.

*Moralizer*

> s conceal the
> uncertain
>
> ties of their–
> own self–super
>
> iority.

## A dialogue

between a less
er-sleep and

the more of
poemed darken

ing self-con
trast

s.


## Off-balanc

ed as if the
ground–itself

had not e
qualled its

own inadequate
ly–held

feet-forming.

# Poetry books by David Jaffin

1. **Conformed to Stone,** Abelard-Schuman, New York 1968, London 1970.

2. **Emptied Spaces,** with an illustration by Jacques Lipschitz, Abelard-Schuman, London 1972.

3. **In the Glass of Winter,** Abelard-Schuman, London 1975, with an illustration by Mordechai Ardon.

4. **As One,** The Elizabeth Press, New Rochelle, N. Y. 1975.

5. **The Half of a Circle,** The Elizabeth Press, New Rochelle, N. Y. 1977.

6. **Space of,** The Elizabeth Press, New Rochelle, N. Y. 1978.

7. **Preceptions,** The Elizabeth Press, New Rochelle, N. Y. 1979.

8. **For the Finger's Want of Sound,** Shearsman Plymouth, England 1982.

9. **The Density for Color,** Shearsman Plymouth, England 1982.

10. **Selected Poems** with an illustration by Mordechai Ardon, English/Hebrew, Massada Publishers, Givatyim, Israel 1982.

11. **The Telling of Time,** Shearsman Books, Kentisbeare, England 2000 and Johannis, Lahr, Germany.

12. **That Sense for Meaning,** Shearsman Books, Kentisbeare, England 2001 and Johannis, Lahr, Germany.

13. **Into the timeless Deep,** Shearsman Books, Kentisbeare, England 2003 and Johannis, Lahr, Germany.

14. **A Birth in Seeing,** Shearsman Books, Exeter, England 2003 and Johannis, Lahr, Germany.

15. **Through Lost Silences,** Shearsman Books, Exeter, England 2003 and Johannis, Lahr, Germany.

16. **A voiced Awakening,** Shearsman Books, Exter, England 2004 and Johannis, Lahr, Germany.

17. **These Time-Shifting Thoughts**, Shearsman Books, Exeter, England 2005 and Johannis, Lahr, Germany.

18. **Intimacies of Sound,** Shearsman Books, Exeter, England 2005 and Johannis, Lahr, Germany.

19. **Dream Flow** with an illustration by Charles Seliger, Shearsman Books, Exeter, England 2006 and Johannis, Lahr, Germany.

20. **Sunstreams** with an illustration by Charles Seliger, Shearsman Books, Exeter, England 2007 and Johannis, Lahr, Germany.

21. **Thought Colors,** with an illustration by Charles Seliger, Shearsman Books, Exeter, England 2008 and Johannis, Lahr, Germany.

22. **Eye-Sensing,** Ahadada, Tokyo, Japan and Toronto, Canada 2008.

23. **Wind-phrasings,** with an illustration by Charles Seliger, Shearsman Books, Exeter, England 2009 and Johannis, Lahr, Germany.

24. **Time shadows,** with an illustration by Charles Seliger, Shearsman Books, Exeter, England 2009 and Johannis, Lahr, Germany.

25. **A World mapped-out,** with an illustration by Charles Seliger, Shearsman Books, Exeter, England 2010.

26. **Light Paths,** with an illustration by Charles Seliger, Shearsman Books, Exeter, England 2011 and Edition Wortschatz, Schwarzenfeld, Germany.

27. **Always Now,** with an illustration by Charles Seliger, Shearsman Books, Bristol, England 2012 and Edition Wortschatz, Schwarzenfeld, Germany.

28. **Labyrinthed,** with an illustration by Charles Seliger, Shearsman Books, Bristol, England 2012 and Edition Wortschatz, Schwarzenfeld, Germany.

29. **The Other Side of Self,** with an illustration by Charles Seliger, Shearsman Books, Bristol, England 2012 and Edition Wortschatz, Schwarzenfeld, Germany.

30. **Light Sources,** with an illustration by Charles Seliger, Shearsman Books, Bristol, England 2013 and Edition Wortschatz, Schwarzenfeld, Germany.

31. **Landing Rights,** with an illustration by Charles Seliger, Shearsman Books, Bristol, England 2014 and Edition Wortschatz, Schwarzenfeld, Germany.

32. **Listening to Silence,** with an illustration by Charles Seliger, Shearsman Books, Bristol, England 2014 and Edition Wortschatz, Schwarzenfeld, Germany.

33. **Taking Leave,** with an illustration by Mei Fêng, Shearsman Books, Bristol, England 2014 and Edition Wortschatz, Schwarzenfeld, Germany.

34. **Jewel Sensed,** with an illustration by Paul Klee, Shearsman Books, Bristol, England 2015 and Edition Wortschatz, Schwarzenfeld, Germany.

35. **Shadowing Images**, with an illustration by Pieter de Hooch, Shearsman Books, Bristol, England 2015 and Edition Wortschatz, Schwarzenfeld.

Book on David Jaffin's poetry: Warren Fulton, **Poemed on a beach,** Ahadada, Tokyo, Japan and Toronto, Canada 2010.